The
Challenged
Population

The Challenged *Population*

Understanding Intellectually and Developmentally Challenged Individuals

Abdul H. Gabisi

THE CHALLENGED POPULATION
Understanding Intellectually and Developmentally Challenged Individuals

iUniverse books may be ordered through booksellers or by contacting:

iUniverse
1663 Liberty Drive
Bloomington, IN 47403
www.iuniverse.com
1-800-Authors (1-800-288-4677)

ISBN: 978-1-4917-8939-1 (sc)
ISBN: 978-1-4917-8938-4 (e)

Library of Congress Control Number: 2016905755

Print information available on the last page.

iUniverse rev. date: 10/18/2016

Contents

Acknowledgments

I sincerely acknowledged the support of my workmates, who were willing to contribute, as resource persons in whatever way they could, when I approached them on this subject. Special acknowledgement to Madam Colleen Quinn, Mrs. Doris Williams-Kanu and all the parents of children of the challenged population who had the courage, empathy and fortitude to give their invaluable experiences, hence, authenticating this work.

Also, I give thanks to the managerial staff of care giving agencies-who wanted to remain anonymous-who made their contribution and fired me up to write from the beginning. Also, members of Institutions very much related to the challenged population, who made their own personal comments hence, helped me in making informed conclusion with regards certain issues.

Further acknowledgement goes to individuals, particularly Dr. S. Sannoh and others, who gave me technical support and equally important, the needed moral support. They boosted my spirit and gave invaluable advice that did help me to make this literature a reality. Though some preferred anonymity, I do thank the following for their support namely, Doreen, Fatmata Rogers, Suliaman, Florence, Billor, and Miniratu Coker. These individuals reaffirmed in me their belief to see this book to its successful completion.

I give thanks as well, to those who actively gave meaningful technical contributions, by responding to phone calls, surveys and scheduled interviews. My profound gratitude goes to the invaluable work placed in the media and the internet, of which some have been listed in my references. Further acknowledgement and gratitude for the financial assistance received and family members, Hashim, Abi, Sufyan, Ajara, Ayesatu, Fatmata and others who gave the needed support.

My wife, Zainab and children, Abdul and Ayesatu who were there to support and patiently worked with me till this exercise became complete. Finally, thanks go to my creator who gave me the will and sustenance to transform this idea into what I have here today.

Summary

The primary aim of this book is to give a meaningful overview of the population of intellectually and developmentally challenged individuals. It includes youths in their twenties to adults as old as their late seventies. The book describes how this population coexists with the "normal" population. You will read about their experiences in group homes and stories of some who journeyed from institutions to assisted homes. I also tell the story of how I became employed in this type of work and what my early experiences in the homes of some of these individuals were.

As the book progresses, I give information on these individuals' homes, continuing with their day programs and ways they are educated. Then I give a background on how the agencies work and how all the important support systems of this population interact. I take the time to give background facts to the readers about how these support systems function.

Also, I depict the manner in which these individuals' parents relate to them, along with the primary workforce, the direct support professionals (DSPs), that assists them. I say much about the merits of the CP, and I discuss the wider spectrum of people in the CP.

Also, the importance of the residential counselors (RCs), DSPs, and residential specialists—as they are interchangeably called in the lives of the individually challenged, consumers, and CP, as they are also known—is brought to the forefront. If these concerns and challenges of the caregivers are not properly addressed or reconciled with, this will definitely affect the quality of life the CP eventually receives.

Though the advocates help to influence change, the final onus for comprehensive change lies with the government. I also take the time to make the reader understand that we are basically a part of this population. I show a clear depiction of the challenged domain. The mentally ill, blind, deaf and dumb, geriatric population, accidentally physically and mentally challenged, and, of course, our veterans are all part of this big picture.

I will often depict that the CP is an extraordinary group of people who have demonstrated their talents and exceptional degrees of fortitude, resilience, and courage to live their lives despite the odds against them. Hence their inclusion to society, by whatever means, should be our collective responsibility.

Chapter 1

Introduction

It is true that only close association with an entity will bring out its correct value. This is accurate from my personal interaction with this part of our population, the CP. One hopes that this book will help to bridge the understanding of the CP and normal community, so to speak.

By definition, CP here refers to individuals from the ages of young adults to senior citizens who have physical and/or mental disabilities. Indeed I am not writing a profound literature of the medical issues, prognoses, or diagnoses that are prevalent among this CP. Neither will I endeavor to give an in-depth report of the medical ailments that define this group.

Furthermore, this writing does not primarily delve into the chronological history of how this CP started, particularly in the United States. Thus I detail how it has evolved over the past six decades and more. I will make some references to give the readers a vivid understanding of this population. This narration is from a few mentally challenged and disabled individuals who started working in basements of churches and living in family homes. They have presently expanded to being housed under the umbrella of established agencies, each with an average of twenty residential homes, depicting the journey traversed by this population.

From the Department of Developmental Disability (DDD) here in New Jersey, funded services and supports are offered in the community by more than 250 New Jersey provider agencies and five residential centers.[1]

In addition, from the 1970s to today, tremendous development has taken place within the ancillary support areas. This is seen from infrastructure to technical innovations to a much more positive change

---

[1] http://www.state.nj.us/humanservices/ddd/home.

of policies, regulations, and laws enacted by the government. These enactments have been through the Department of Human Services (DHS) with great influence from advocacy networks, agencies servicing the CP, and general public.

The thrust of this writing will primarily address the experiences of the consumers themselves and their direct support groups, namely the following:

- **The primary support network**: This is their parents and guardians and/or professional help, particularly the RCs or DSPs, nurses, and entire support system referred to as "the agency." This body has the sole responsibility of organizing and providing the provisions for consumers to be properly assimilated into our established society.
- **The secondary support establishment:** This includes the transportation department, technical services, and DHS, in which we have Division of Developmental Disabilities (DDD). They oversee the life journeys of the entire CP on behalf of the government.
- **Training, research, and other entities that work toward improving the livelihood of the CP:** These include the Elizabeth Boggs Center, Matheny Medical and Educational Center, University of Medical and Dentistry of New Jersey, the advocacy networks, and Therap.

Interestingly, these segments are actively engaged in assimilating the CP into our normal population. Hopefully the experiences stated here will make the reader have a profound understanding of this CP.

The CP is generally comprised of individuals from normal family settings, friends, and society at large. Basically they are one of us. The sooner members in the community begin to understand the CP, the easier their full potential will be realized, thus enhancing their integration and assimilation into society.

Furthermore, members of the general population will better appreciate life and virtues such as empathy, love, patience, and self-worth, as they all relate with the CP. Incidentally, the role of the primary support team will be properly appreciated, particularly by individuals and groups outside the support system of the CP.

The CP are specifically challenged with physical and mental issues. They are usually nonambulatory or wheelchair bound, or they may use walkers. Common mental challenges are usually mild mental retardation, cerebral palsy, autism, bipolar, cognitive disabilities, spina bifida, dyslexia, brain injury, and behavioral issues.

Some people have disproportionately viewed the CP heavily alongside other socioeconomic challenges that are equally inherent in our society. Just like poverty, insecurity and lack of basic amenities impede development in certain parts of the world, so the physical and mental disabilities should be viewed. With this positive approach, neither will be viewed as a plague, a misfit of our society, but moreover, a strong sense of purpose will be borne by all to change our society for the best.

Interestingly, in delving into the CP, one identifies a sector of the population that could be qualified as CP due to accidents and, to a lesser extent, diseases. These individuals, in the course of living a normal life, by sheer fate, became physically and sometimes mentally disabled. Though they are not the primary category referred to, their population has given a positive complexion to the CP. This possible transformation by fate has helped the normal population to realize how they can become part of the CP. It's a position the individual challenged became by natural occurrence, not by accident or choice.

Not only is the driving motive in writing this book to complement the immense efforts carried out to positively project the CP; it is to have a literature that will picture how the CP exist on a holistic (universal) level. The search for a book that would comprehensively address the coexistence of the CP, as defined earlier with our normal society, further propelled me to make this contribution. Again, I selected the young adults up to the early seniors, primarily because that is the domain I have directly engaged with.

I have injected much lighthearted material into these experiences, which, though based on true incidents, will help the reader to understand the CP.

Chapter 2

Early Experiences with the Challenged Population

"Working in a production plant."

I came into the caregiving field when I decided to improve my finances, a situation that all of us may share. I had been in the United States for a year, and I was fortunate to have a job related to my engineering profession at home, working in an extrusion production plant. As a quality inspector, I had to do the best part of my eight-hour shift making sure the specifications and tolerances of the plastic window frames were okay.

This work is fun for the first hour, but being at it for the eight-hour work period is quite an ordeal. Amid Bakarr a country man of mine, told me how I could be gainfully employed in the caregiving field. Considering my financial situation, I concluded this additional employment would be worth investigating.

The next day, after completing my day's work at the production plant, I was truly exhausted and ready to go home and rest. However, Amid convinced me to visit this proposed place of work. Within thirty minutes, we arrived at the main office of the caregiving organization in Milltown, North Brunswick. Here we started their application process.

Within a few weeks, I quickly went through the application for the job. This process includes verifying my competency for the job, checking my background, and completing any other standard employment procedures. Then I completed the orientation process, and I was ready to start work as a RC. My first work site was a residential home in North Brunswick. There I was enthusiastically greeted by two Caucasian men who were in their thirties, Jay and Rick, and two African Americans, Amina and Isaac, who I later learned were staff members.

For the next three hours we interacted, I had a firsthand knowledge of these young men's challenges. Despite all the prep talk and orientation received, I was experiencing it for the first time. The guys were watching their favorite TV programs, and then they had dinner. Later one of the staff called them upstairs to take their medication. It then fully dawned on me that I was at my job site, quite unlike the production plant where I worked, where to chat and interact truly happens during the fifteen-minute break time.

After working in the residential home for a few weeks, I began to understand this unique environment. The residents, sometimes known as our "consumers" and presently called "individual served," became more relaxed. A world I had not been quite exposed to became more revealing, and gradually I could comprehend their challenges and desires to live fulfilled existences.

This house of four male residents each portrays their outlooks on life. Leonard, a smoker, is legally blind, but he has a very sharp mind. One day Commission on Accreditation of Rehabilitation Facilities (CARF) inspectors came to check on the house, a biyearly inspection to ensure these residential homes meet government standards.

I went outside to the porch, where Leonard was smoking, and asked, "What's going on?"

Leonard said, "Abdul, same old thing. Nothing changes." From his perception he sees these officers coming every other year and performing routine stuff.

The youngest and strongest, Rick, is very affectionate. We take the men to the community to eat, watch movies or baseball games, or simply do some personal shopping. There Rick makes friends during those community visits.

The other two, Jay and Charles, love music and are very interested in the opposite sex. Charles had a lady friend from another agency whom he befriended at his day program. Jay had a girlfriend from the same agency. Incidentally, he had a rival, an issue that was very tricky to resolve. It was quite an interesting love tango, which, with responsible supervision, much drama was prevented.

One gratifying memory was these four guys helping to enrich the others' lives through the interaction they had with one another. Jay and Leonard loved the Beatles, while Elvis Presley was solely Jay's guy. He adored Elvis so much that every afternoon one would hear him blasting his music for at least an hour.

Later I had to work in other homes and eventually left the very agency for another. Indeed I severed contact with them for some years. One day I drove by North Brunswick and decided to see them. It was quite a good feeling to see Jay's warm, spontaneous response. He enthusiastically greeted me, not forgetting my name. He was able to remember the interesting time we shared together.

Jay spoke about his love life. I sadly learned that Leonard, who used to love having a giant size of any item, had passed away. Charles, whom I used to take occasionally to his girlfriend's place, had moved to another residential home. The same was the case with Rick.

Jay was now the only one left with three new inmates. We spoke about their trips to Quick Check at Highland Park, where they all went for their personal shopping. I can still see that smile on his face as I was bidding him good-bye.

This spontaneous, warm response I received from Jay is very common with these guys. Most recently I visited one of the employment centers after I'd been absent for about a year. They welcomed me with such empathy. This makes the CP stand out as a unique group who appreciate people, have immense gratitude, and love mankind.

Jamesburg Group Home

If North Brunswick could be considered my very first experience with the CP, I also had unique experiences at Jamesburg Group Home. Unlike North Brunswick Group Home, Jamesburg Group Home had a mix of both male and female residents living in a ranch house. The two males, Bob and Tom, shared the house with Frances, Martha, and Princess, who were all in wheelchairs.

Tom, a relatively independent, heavyset man, was quite a likeable person. He and Mary, a nonambulatory introvert, were close friends but maintained separate rooms. Their close interaction was responsibly supervised.

During my very first day of working at this house, I was talking with Tom and a staff member when I heard some sound coming from one of the rooms. Truly I was wondering what that unfamiliar sound was. I observed the other members in the living room were quite comfortable with it. Later I learned this was how Frances expressed herself. Also, Bob, who loved playing his guitar, made a similar sound as a way of expressing his peaceful mood.

If one would have walked into the house without being briefed on how this group of the CP expressed themselves, one would have definitely been perplexed. However, all this continues to teach us how different we are.

Family Members

The other source of early, firsthand experience came from employees who had blood relations with the disabled. This bond is very strong, and of course their empathy with the CP will be considered the strongest.

Fortunately, I interacted well with this category of individuals. Very early contact came from Madam Doris Williams, also an employee of the agency. The other individuals I met previously had mixed associations. Some of these parents worked in the agency with their children within. Or in other instances, their children were in other agencies.

Finally there were the many family members whose children or siblings were our consumers. Incidentally these family members were usually moms. Seldom were others siblings of our consumers. Not often did we have dads be a part of this family group. Later I will discuss moms I worked with whose children were also in these agencies. Their contributions greatly helped to shape the understanding of the CP.

Madam Williams has one child Shavaunda, who is nonambulatory with mild retardation. I worked with her in this field for over five years and could still feel the compassion she had for our challenged individuals. She related to them as her own children.

Working with her enhanced my relation to the individual challenged. I happened to work with Madam Williams in taking the consumers on community visits, which was always interesting. We went to Atlantic City and Manville Dance and participated in such simple treats as getting them a haircut in the neighborhood.

One issue that impacted me was how Madam Williams' disabled child interacted with her other siblings, who were all ambulatory and functional in the society. She was treated very normally, and she coped well with her challenges, which was much more physical than mental.

One day I visited this family, and not long after Shavaunda came home from work. She alighted from the bus and was transferred to her wheelchair. They drove her to the house, and she conveniently got herself from the wheelchair to the flight of stairs leading to the first floor. She held a friendly conversation with me while slowly getting herself through the stairs.

I did admire her fortitude as she ascended the stairs to her room. I recently learned she had been given a rail stair lift, which is much comfortable to use. I wish her and others in her challenged position do receive more of this assistance as they graciously journey through life.

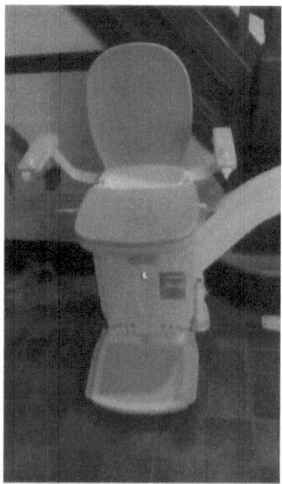 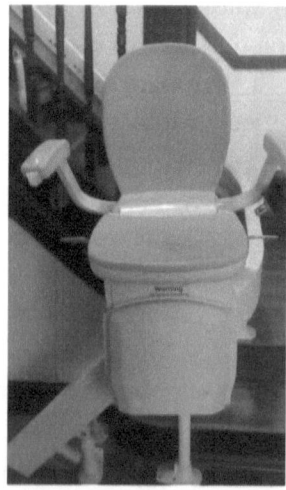

"Shavaunda Acorn Stair rail."

In fact she was quite cheerful, and she later became a supervisor at her workplace. Also, every year, she goes on a camping trip, a short vacation that most of these challenged individuals embark on. Some go to Miami, Las Vegas, and other exotic resorts around the United States.

Close association with the challenged individuals makes one experience how his or her loved ones relate to him or her. Generally they could be divided into three categories:

- The first parents stay with their individually challenged child or children despite the day-to-day challenges they will have to go through. An example of that was Madam Williams and other loving moms, as one later reads through the book.
- The second category puts them in group homes but visits regularly or asks they come for home visits. They also interact well with RCs and those who work with their children. An example of such special mom is Mrs. Jones, mother of Paul of South Wood Group Home. Mrs. Jones is an awesome mom who is very appreciative of the assistance given to her only son. She willingly gives presents to the entire staff during Christmas and supports us with our group home parties. Though not obligated, she insisted on buying video games, which the other residents could use along with Paul. I could still remember her coming regularly on a weekly basis to visit Paul in the home.
- The third category hardly interacts with them and rarely makes calls or interacts with the agency. I'm not passing judgment. They have their reasons for interacting with them this way. Sadly some of these challenged individuals had given their parents or guardians very traumatic moments that led to this arrangement.

Special Moments

During the early days of interaction, two issues surfaced, which overtime rescinded into oblivion. First, the RC, residential specialist, or DSP adjusts to his or her role in supporting the consumers. One Saturday morning I came to relieve an overnight female staff member, Samantha, at North Brunswick Group Home and saw a comical situation but an issue of concern. Both staff and consumer were going in circles around the group home van parked on the premises of the home.

The consumer Rick, who was six-foot-two and weighed 245 pounds, was pursuing the overnight staff lady, who was a petite lady standing five-foot-four and weighing 125 pounds. I had to redirect him to go to his room and later counsel him for behaving inappropriately. Though the incident should have been stopped earlier, the scene was somehow comical. Rick was usually a docile person. At this time he was simply upset for not having his choice granted.

Once staff has adjusted with a consumer, the bond made continues to strengthen with time. The training acquired and high frequency of meetings make positive adjustments happen within a short time. To reinforce this here is a case in point.

I once worked with an agency, Development Rock Agency, which housed two independent consumers in regular apartments and assigned one DSP to supervise them during their eight-hour work shift. That Monday evening shift, I was assigned to work in apartment eleven and scheduled to supervise Victor and Alfred. I arrived there at three, and twenty minutes later Victor arrived in the apartment from his day program.

Seeing me for the first time in the apartment with no prior notice from a known staff did not sit well with him. Despite the niceties exchanged to put him at ease, he prowled around for a while and asked if we could visit his mates at apartment seventeen a few blocks down the road. Knowing he was trying to confirm I was his assigned staff, I complied with his wish, and soon we were to apartment seventeen.

There his mates warmly greeted us, and he saw how enthusiastically they related to me. After some time he told me we could return to his apartment. I smiled and joked with him if he were now comfortable to work with me. He smiled and tried to apologize for bringing me to apartment seventeen, but I told him I fully understood his apprehension. Since then we have been good friends, and sometimes he prompts me to narrate the story. This short episode clearly tells us that the CP, particularly the relatively independent individuals, is fully aware of their environment, even if their ways of responding might be different from ours.

In another situation I observed how individuals outside the CP respond to us and the consumers. The level of acceptance is actually felt when the CP steps out of their domain. However, every time this outside contact is established, as DSPs, our level of understanding and ability in professionally handling the situation increases.

Better still the normal population acceptance for the CP increases with having more interaction. This happens when we take one consumer on a community visit or in relatively large groups to movies, restaurants, and parks. Also, there are the visits they make to their regular doctors' appointments.

An incident occurred in Quick Check, Highland Park, where we go every Friday evening to buy personal items for them. Because of their frequency of visits, the Quick Check's staff and their regulars know them. However, on that fateful day, Charles jumped the queue he was in to pay for his items, and the staff redirected him to return to his original position. Though he was acting up, the customers were quite understandable with the situation and displayed a reasonable degree of tolerance toward us.

On other occasions they are out in the community but predominantly interacting with their own. My early experience was going to the Manville Dance, which takes place every Monday evening at the Manville Veterans of Foreign Wars Center. The first time we attended the dance with our four guys from North Brunswick Group Home, it was quite an experience.

Interestingly enough, after just being in the United States for a few years, I noticed the Manville Dance was similar to our nightclub settings back home. I have been to house parties and other social gatherings, but still not visited nightclubs here.

At the Manville Dance, I relived the experience again. So many group home vehicles were parked outside, and one independent consumer was assisting with the parking. At the entrance we paid and entered the dance floor, which other consumers, DSPs, and support members partially filled up. The consumers were having a great time dancing and having fun. They expressed themselves the best way they could. Both ambulatory and nonambulatory were having fun with no exceptions.

Some were very well dressed with a purpose, either to impress or get a date. The venue was a discotheque with a DJ blasting their favorite music. These songs were the same current music that youths in the States listen and dance to. At eight, there was a short intermission, and drinks were served, courtesy of the house. After that the dance resumed, and thereafter members started dispersing to their various homes. It is great to know that the dance party constitutes a very broad spectrum of consumers from different agencies in most counties of New Jersey.

The Building on the left is where "Manville dance", organized for the challenged population, take place most Mondays for the past twenty years plus. The property located at 600 Washington Avenue Manville, NJ 08835 is owned by the Veterans of Manville Inc.

The Veterans Memorial Hall is a 7200 Square Foot wood floored facility and can accommodate 400 people. Interestingly on most Monday evenings the parking lots is usually filled up with vehicles of service providers whilst inside is bustling with a cross section of the CP and friends having a good time.

Chapter 3

Residential Home Experiences

"A regular Group Home"

Many decades ago consumers would stay with their family members. Later as this population grew, institutions were established as premises and day programs for these challenged individuals. Over the years development took place, allowing the CP to have more options regarding the places they live and ways they would be integrated into the normal population.

It would be interesting to know how the present-day group home settings for our consumers evolved. Institutionalization of people with disability constituted of two parts: the mental health disabilities and intellectual and developmental disabilities. Seventeen seventy-three marked the beginning of the mental health.

The institutionalization for people with intellectual and developmental disabilities has been influenced more by economic factors than the political one dealt with by those of the Mental Health Department (MHD). The reality is that economic pressures were making it more difficult for families to continue educating or caring for family members on their own.

These schools became boarding schools, and slowly economic interest undermined the need to provide education and placement in employment in the community. Again the pressure of containing this population from 1800–1900 caused these institutions in the United States to rise from a little over four thousand to fifteen thousand.[2]

After this trend continued, economic interests and the need to reintegrate this population to our normal population brought about the process of deinstitutionalization of the intellectually and developmentally disabled population. Parents realized their children had few rights and seemed removed from mainstream society.

In places like Canada, in 1953, parents like the Russells and other fearless families did contribute toward taking their children from institutions to bringing them home to ensure they lived closer to the community. The United Nations recognized this trend in 1969, and in June 1996 most of the large institutions for people with developmental disabilities were closed. An example is the Rosewood Center, an institution for people with developmental disabilities.[3]

Also, very comprehensive studies were done regarding deinstitutionalization and community living intellectual disability services in Scandinavia, Britain, and the United States.[4] This trend continues to this day in New Jersey and has nevertheless brought concern to the smooth transition of consumers from institutions to present-day group homes. Regarding their homes, the setting changed into three distinct categories:

1. The challenged individual stays with his or her family or guardian and goes to day programs alongside other activities in the community.
2. Individuals who own residential homes accommodate the consumers with financial assistance from the government.
3. Agencies have become a well-organized body that provide full services for the CP.

---

[2] Savannah Logsdon-Breakstone.
[3] Jesse Bering, "A Forgotten Scandal in Baltimore's High Society," *Medical Examiner*, March 17, 2014.
[4] Edited by Jim Mansell, University of Kent at Canterbury, and Kent Ericsson, University of Uppsala.

Agency services are continually approved by the government, who incidentally provide 90 percent of the cost. Additional financial support comes from philanthropists and other fund-raising activities. Also included in this list are individuals who are serviced by supportive living.

Again the consumers are truly the residents of these residential homes. These homes are usually single homes or a large building divided into one- or two-unit apartments. Here in the state of New Jersey, there are over two hundred and fifty agencies with some having over fifteen residential homes.[5]

To ensure this CP is truly integrated to the community, the state here in New Jersey created this arrangement. New Jersey Department of Community Affairs (NJDCA), New Jersey Housing and Mortgage Financing Agency (NJHMFA), and New Jersey Department of Human services (NJDHS) crafted Special Needs Housing Partnership Loan Program (SNHPLP). As part of the SNHPLP initiative, they help create housing for the CP by utilizing monies in the municipal Affordable Housing Trust Fund (AHTF) accounts.[6] Also, for detailed information on SNHPLP, readers can visit the NJHMFA's website.[7]

This above provision created by the government does complement the ongoing services being carried out by the established agencies providing homes for the CP. Thus our individually served, the CP, have the opportunity to practically integrate in the community.

As stated earlier, the agency I worked for had physically and mentally challenged persons. A percentage of the consumers are in wheelchairs, others have walkers, and a relative few are regarded as independent individuals. These independent consumers, with respect to their peers, are not as physically challenged and have more coping skills than their cohorts. Fortunately having worked with these individuals, I knew their potential to some extent and ways they utilize them.

In this particular South Wood Group Home, the three males— Kennedy, Harold, and Donald—were ambulatory while Harry and John were not. Incidentally they were all nonverbal individuals. Harry

---

5   www.state.nj.us/humanservices/ddd/home.
6   www.state.nj.us/dca/services/residents/housing.html.
7   www.state.nj.us/dca/hmfa/developers/needs/partnership.

and John had manual wheelchairs usually placed by the side of their beds when they finally retired to their room.

I can recall how Harry and Donald would get dressed. The first time I tried to get them dressed was very challenging. The next time I allowed them to assist me, and the task was quickly done. Though they were nonambulatory and nonverbal, I gradually related to them by their gestures and the unique sounds they made.

At the dining table, they can mostly feed themselves with the assistance of special tableware (spoons, table knives, and forks). Again when summer comes by, they make the most use of their compound. These guys enjoy being around the garden that the group home staff cultivated from scratch. We worked with them, played basketball, and barbecued as well.

In consultation with the agency, our house worked with three other residential homes in the region and had a group barbecue. Staff and consumers had fun time. These moments enhanced the relationship between staff and consumers. The agency's newsletter did a great job in announcing this event to other members in the agency.

Indeed the agency makes it their concern to celebrate our consumers' birthdays. Also, with the input from parents, this became much fun. It was more exciting when we had consumers' families attending these house parties, along with the birthday person's boyfriend or girlfriend in attendance. There is food, music, and a lot of empathy going on. Staff members do have their favorite consumers, and at the end of the day, we all share in with the jokes and laughter.

Other times the parents do ask that their child do come to their homes. There, they make a great party for them, inviting quite a cross section of their families and friends. In this setting, staff gets to know the family members better, helping to relate more with the birthday person, our consumer.

Generally our consumers do have their special friends, and this has been forged through many ways. At the Jamesburg Group Home, both individuals lived in the same homes but at separate ends of the building, and their meetings were supervised. In another group home, they lived in the same compound but in a separate building. These individuals were quite independent and played an active part in their self-advocacy groups. Again we had individuals living in the same agency but different group homes, along with individuals living in two different agencies.

In the case of individuals living in two different groups home was that of Charles in North Brunswick Group Home and his girlfriend Jane living in Olive Group Home in Somerset. They nurtured their romantic relationship at their day program, and as they grew fond of each other, the desire to share their time grew. Charles always reminded me of their supervised visits, which the two group homes did well in executing. In other instances Charles reminded staff of making phone calls to his girlfriend.

In all the described relations, they share gifts, express their emotions, and sometimes go on camp trips/vacations. Essentially these consumers get up in the morning after a good night's rest and get prepared for their day programs or doctors' appointments. On returning home they either relax in their rooms or come and spend time on the porch or in the living room. Depending on their monthly activity chart, they go out and interact with the community. Later they have their dinner, which is done with a properly made monthly menu.

They have evening activities, which also are properly designed to include their individual goals. One quite independent consumer gave much input into his evening activities. Staff used to call him "consumer specialist" for his ability to come up with so many activities. Indeed he facilitated consumers getting out to the community, even though his frequency was on the high side.

Among community activities were taking consumers for dinner at IHOP, Hometown Buffet, or Red Lobster. Also, they go bowling, watch baseball games, and attend movies at cinemas. They also carry out their personal banking and shopping. When it comes to general house shopping, they are well incorporated by helping with the list and joining in doing the shopping.

In certain agencies where the individually challenged are highly functional, they secure regular jobs in the community. They usually go to their jobs during the day or in the evening, just as we have varying shifts and work schedules. Some have job coaches working with them, and for the uninformed public, they truly blend with the rest of the workforce of society.

In another group home, precisely Mountain Group Home, six male residents lived there. The oldest, seventy-five-year-old Marcus is ambulatory and verbal with mental retardation. At this age he still could remember presidents of his time, which include Presidents Ronald Reagan, Franklin D. Roosevelt, Harry Truman, Dwight D. Eisenhower, and Richard Nixon, and he still knows President Barack Obama is our current administrator.

One peculiar thing is assisting him with dressing. He will definitely help, and if by chance you do try to place his garment or footwear in a wrong position, he will surely correct you. He used to sing the national anthem very well, but with time the words faded away. Now and again, considering his aging situation, he surprises us by making sharp outbursts. However, his stubbornness—or rather restlessness—is increasing.

On some nights Papa Marcus could be up for the entire period, and how he musters this energy is unbelievable. No amount of redirection will get him to stay in bed. Staff usually assists him with his personal hygiene and try to keep him from making his loud, disconcerting outburst. Unfortunately this affects his peers, thus disturbing their peace. Staff nevertheless do their utmost to deescalate the moment.

Harrison also is ambulatory and verbal with mild mental disabilities. He exhibits the traits of a savant, having an incredible mental memory. He is the encyclopedia for his peers. As such, he could accurately recall their birthdays and holidays and tell when the garbage or recycling bins are to be taken out and even when they have doctors' appointments for all of them.

In fact every morning at breakfast table, his peers will ask him about the day's itinerary. He is very reliable on those issues, so he is very helpful to the house. If the house food inventory is running low, he will definitely inform staff.

Rick, ambulatory but nonverbal, is very easygoing. He could sense empathy and demonstrate that with gratitude, particularly when his mom comes to pick him up for his regular weekend home visits. He loves listening to music in the morning, and black-and-white production movies are his favorites.

On the other hand, Johnny, ambulatory and verbal, can be at times aggressive, particularly to the female sex. He likes intimidating female staff by pulling their hair and has never-ending questions that he knows the answers. Knowing him, this is how he communicates with people.

Victor, also ambulatory and verbal, moves slowly, much so with the weight he bears. Staff encourages him to exercise in the morning and constantly watch his diet. He loves his Sunday service where he participates by singing and considering himself very much part of the congregation.

He feels very good about himself, so after dressing every morning, he will compliment himself. Music is his passion, so where the words are missing, he will come up with his own. They generally do love music, and every morning they will request staff to have music during breakfast. With this atmosphere they will hold their lighthearted conversation.

Peter, ambulatory and verbal, is a meticulous person. He helps with the laundry and lunch preparation and has a thing for cutting coupons. A hyperactive person, he is very cooperative with staff. He also writes notes, like keeping his personal journal. Interestingly this is one way he communicates with staff and management. One time at the home, a new staff member was hired and, as always, had to be oriented with the consumers and residence as a whole. It took him a while to realize that Peter, though independent, requires assistance from staff.

On a typical weekday, one will have a conversation like this going on during breakfast time. In the dining room, Harrison, who had previously helped with breakfast, is already seated in his usual seat, with Rick on his left and Peter on his right. They all maintain their regular seating positions. Also, Victor is at one end of the head table.

Known for his love for food, he is also seated. He smiles and says, "Hardy, I look handsome."

I take a good look at him and say, "Great. But do not forget to reverse your shoe positions."

Victor replies, "Okay." Then he starts eating his breakfast.

Rick comes walking to his seat by Harrison. He sits down but points to the radio, uttering the words "Ba ba bah." I smile and walk to turn on the radio.

At this time Peter is now seated opposite Victor in the opposite head chair. In a cheerful mood, he says, "Hardy, good morning. The coffee tastes good."

I say, "Good morning, Peter. Guess you slept well."

Peter replies, "Oh, yes, Hardy. I did."

I move now to Marcus to assist with his breakfast. At this point Johnny, sitting next to Marcus, directly opposite Rick, starts with his wave of questions. "Harrison, today is what day? Do I have to go to work?"

Harrison, in his short but accurate outburst, replies, "Today is Monday. You do work at your day program."

At this point they all will continue with questions for Harrison, who keeps giving them the correct answers.

At this time I am about done with helping Marcus with his breakfast. I look at Harrison and ask, "Harrison, why are you not properly dressed for your day program?"

Harrison replies, "Hardy, today I have a ten thirty appointment with my primary physician, and Abe will be taking me."

I thank him, and we return to the day's routine activities.

For the time I have interacted with them, despite their challenges, they earnestly look forward to living their lives to the fullest. They love going to their day programs. After eating their breakfast, they go to the living room, where they wait for the bus. There you will observe them reminding us about the bus arrival.

Sometimes we have false outbursts from Marcus. "Oh, the bus is here!"

A correction from Harrison follows. Finally when the bus arrives, they will put on their coats with staff assistance, enthusiastically pick up their lunches, and walk to the bus. The lady bus driver, Jenifer, greets them cheerfully and then directs them to their seats.

They also attend the agency programs, such as their walkathon, a very productive program. Consumers and members of the agency, much so those from residential homes, engage in this activity to socialize, exercise, and generate needed funds for the agency. This financial help is gaining much significance with the increased challenge in getting funds from the state.

Consumers' participation in the Special Olympics is also a very important event for them. This is their Olympics, and every year prospective consumers undergo their training. DSPs help with their preparation. At the end of the Special Olympics, successful athletes come home with their medals. During that week they proudly wear their medals, be it gold, silver, or bronze. They wear it to their day program and events taking place, feeling very proud about their achievements.

Generally as in all residential homes, staff do give all the necessary support to ensure the individually served consumers live a much fulfilled life. This starts from their life in a very hygienic surrounding, followed by a complete caring for their personal hygiene and having their required food with the administration of their medication.

At this juncture readers should be reminded that what transpires here in Mountain Group Home is quite similar to other group homes. In addition, the character of the individual bears similarities to this CP. A case in point is this particular one.

A picnic was organized for several group homes of Volta Agency on July 4 and was well attended both by consumers and staff. By all social measurement, the picnic was a success. Consumers, family members, and staff, including management, interacted as one big family. There was food and drinks, and fun games charged the vicinity. Naturally there were a few incidents, but with timely interventions, the situations were quickly deescalated.

During my course of interaction, I did see how this large family was a true representation of consumers from Mountain Group Home, South Wood Group Home, and other group homes who service these segments of our CP. I saw the likes of Victor, Harrison, and Johnny. Indeed let me say something of the last two.

A consumer with the behavioral character of Johnny is quite a challenge. Several times staff had to intervene to calm him down. This subtly reminded us of our population but made us more proactive to meet the moments. Hence the picnic continued with a sense of comradeship, the ingredient of its success.

The other consumer, Bob, shared the savant characteristic of Harrison. Incidentally Bob was introduced to me by Brother Savage, a staff from his group home. Indeed this awesome, gentle man reaffirmed the potentials that are inherent in this CP.

Bob is essentially a working encyclopedia. From local politicians to state and national, he could tell you their names. Furthermore, if you name a country on the planet, he will tell you its leader as well as the capital city. During the time we interacted, I was impressed by the professorial demeanor he exhibited, which most would not credit to our CP. Imagine what a performance we would have if these incredible abilities of our CP are properly showcased to the universal population.

With respect to our residential group homes, nurses do ensure the monthly menu prepared meets the dietary prescriptions or requirements of each consumer. Also, training programs do incorporate how staff could adequately meet with these services. Furthermore, this process ensures that adequate provision is made for their integration into society at large, hence giving them the opportunity to make personal choices to carry out their lives to the fullest.

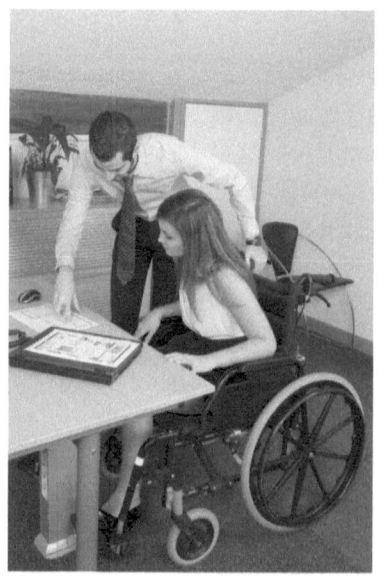

For the above to be successfully accomplished, staff and support system must be fully trained and have the requisite materials to execute these tasks. Policies made by agencies should constantly be reviewed to meet with the current challenges of the day. DSPs should not be placed in situations where caring for the consumers would not ironically make them contradict these very policies. In addition to the checks and balances established by DDD and thus carried out by agencies, the need to have a caring DSP for this CP to live their lives to the fullest cannot be overemphasized.

Interestingly, as the CP shows diverse representation of the human population, so does the supporting workforce. The DSPs or RCs come from diverse backgrounds, but the majority of this workforce constitutes

African Americans with a scattered amount of Asians, Europeans, and Haitians. A high percentage of African Americans come from East and West Africa. Despite the high job turnover rate that is observed in this field, it could be safely said that this demographic picture has a strong correlation of the cultural traits of these nationalities attracted to this profession.

African Americans generally do care for their elders and the disadvantaged population. Despite our earning power, remittances are made home, and the extended family maintained do reflect this trait. Ironically this quality is not shown by some of the leadership of these African American states of origin.

For the CP to have this workforce composition is not an accidental occurrence. Generally this makeup of demographic representation is significantly seen in the caregiving services and progresses to the health and medical field. This is normally the reason why many African Americans are in the fields of nursing, along with other caregiving and medical professions.

"Caregivers embracing diversity."

Chapter 4

The Educational System of the Challenged Population

Interestingly a significant percentage of the population supporting the CP does not properly know this subject, the educational system. Oftentimes, if DSPs, RCs, or residential specialists are asked about the educational system embodying this population, the answer is usually vague. These are usually the reasons for their lack of an educated answer.

Most of the DSPs serve the CP after the consumers have left their schools; hence the DSPs usually do not know how that phase occurred. Individually served consumers, namely our intellectually and developmentally disabled persons, are accepted into residential homes when they are at least twenty-one years old. The CP, as I mentioned earlier, would have already completed their school phase, and the small percentage of consumers engaged in those activities are not in their care.

The other reason is primarily why I am writing. They, like the general populace, don't know what provisions this population have to complete in the educational system. In this regard some members of the CP, despite their challenges, graduate to become very eminent specialists in their field.

In the reference section, I have added a very impressive list of challenged individuals who have—and still contribute toward—the continued development of our human endeavors. They have successfully battled their physical and sometimes intellectual challenges and brilliantly accomplished their scholarly goals.

Their success has given us a profound meaning of resoluteness, fortitude, and the sheer force of an unbroken will to succeed. Names like Mother Teresa, Mozart, Beethoven, Helen Keller, and even Stevie Wonder do come to mind. I will later state some names that do merit belonging on this list.

In order to create a strong sense of inclusiveness, I am including individuals who are challenged but not specifically within the domain of the CP. The awareness they do share strong ties with the CP will further give the readership more reason for embracing this population. In short the spectrum of the general CP is fully depicted.

Several decades ago, as I stated previously, the government thought it necessary to have institutions whereby this population would have adequate education. Members of the CP were usually identified early in regular schools with the need to have special assistance. Through advocacy, special provisions were put in place to enable them to perform alongside their less challenged counterparts. Sometimes special educational institutions were established to meet with their challenged situation, for example, Allegro School, Matheny School and Hospital, and Skyland Center.

The government, through special agencies, helped enact laws, regulations, and policies that today has made this CP very successful with their educational career. ARC, one agency actually formed by parents of the CP, started this educational process in 1950. They wanted their children to have more than just institutional education that were abounding then.[8]

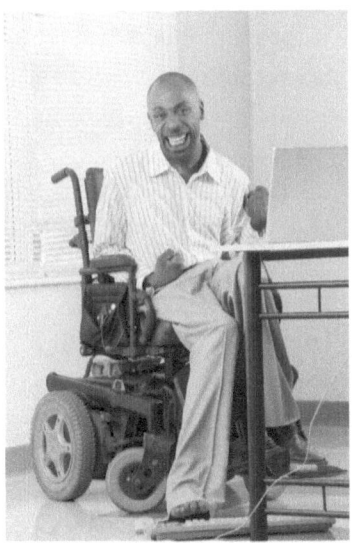

"Education making good of my challenges"

---

[8]   www.thearc.org/who-we-are/history.

Individuals with Disabilities Education Act (IDEA), a federal law first enacted in 1973, ensures that public schools serve educational needs of students with disabilities. Specifically this legislation addresses the educational needs of the disabled and intellectually challenged population. They successfully came up with recommendations that the government, through its special education services, Individualized Education Program (IEP), and Free Appropriate Public Education (FAPE), did help to make this act applicable to all fifty states and American territories. In 2011 more than six million school-aged children in the United States received special education service as a result of IDEA. Also, some 2.2 million are students identified with specific learning disabilities.[9]

The departments, namely the Department of Education and judicial system, have supported and established an educational system that has empowered the CP to successfully pursue their educational goals. Specifically several federal laws are designed to provide rights to children and qualify them for additional protection if they have a learning disability. The Elementary and Secondary Education Act (ESEA), commonly known as No Child Left Behind (NCLB), challenges states and school districts to improve students' academic achievement.[10] Each year Congress appropriates billions of dollars to help support state and local education, research teacher training, technology, and other activities.

Also, it is of use to know that the Americans with Disabilities Amendment Acts (ADAAA) and Section 504 of the Rehabilitation Act improve access to accommodations for students and adults with learning disabilities in schools and workplaces. Section 504 of the Rehabilitation Act of 1973 is a civil right law that prohibits discrimination on the basis of disability in programs and activities, both public and private, that receive federal financial assistance. In January 2009 this protection became broader, giving qualifying students additional support services, auxiliary aids, and/or accommodation in public schools.

Furthermore, though Section 504 does not provide funding for special education or related services, it does permit the federal government to take away funding from programs that do not comply

---

[9] National Center for Learning Disability, www.nlcd.org/disability-advocacy.
[10] Ibid.

with the law. This instrument of compliance has indeed helped the CP to be assured of fulfilling their educational goals. Specifically Princeton Child Development Institute (PCDI), founded in 1971, established a school for autistic children. Special work has been done at this early stage, which helps individuals to have better adult learning.

With the above information, one will have a better understanding of the role our government has played in assuring the CP do have a fair shot at their academic pursuits. Also, with the relentless advocacy entities and general public, the educational opportunities for the CP will continue to improve.

Posteducational Opportunities for the CP

After our CP has gone through some of the educational opportunities provided above, most continue to attend day programs. These programs mainly function as work centers and recreational facilities and seldom as a place for furthering their intellectual goals. The latter is what Madam Quinn strongly believes in. She, with the experience of working with this population for over three decades and having a child in this population, strongly believes this latent potential intrinsic in the consumers could be harnessed.

Years ago, while I was working for some of these group home agencies, some consumers did attend special evening classes for the disabled. Andrew of Jamesburg Group Home did attend banking and other adult subjects at East Brunswick Adult Learning Center. Also, Philip of the same group home did attend some music and computer skills lessons. These learning facilities do continue to enrich the lives of this population and help them fulfill their dreams.

The "people and families magazine "has accomplished a lot in bridging the gap between individuals with developmental disabilities and the general public. The publishers, New Jersey Council on Developmental Disabilities (NJCDD), have successfully used this magazine as an instrument in properly advocating and depicting the activities carried out by this population. Among the many impactful articles that comes to mind is the awareness of our first responders to this population. Their knowledge about the CP, as Jonathan Jaffe wrote in "First to Respond: Sometimes the Last to Know," should help a lot in giving fair treatment to the CP.

Furthermore, as one continues to explore this domain, I realize that our challenged individuals do contribute very significantly in enriching our lives, virtually in all field of human endeavor. Here are a few examples:

- Ron Whyte, a playwright, was on the presidential committee for the employment of the handicapped, the first committee set up at executive level to address formal empowerment of the disabled population regarding significant integration to the public.[11]
- Tony Coelho, a former congressman from California, lived with epilepsy. He did go through the education system, which enabled him to serve as representative for five terms.
- Kathrynne McGee, an American activist, founded the National Association for Down Syndrome. Her daughter Tricia was afflicted with Down syndrome.
- Frieda Zames, a polio victim, became a mathematics professor, writer, and advocate for access to all aspects of public life, especially transportation. She campaigned for wheelchair access on New York City buses, ferries, and taxis and buildings like the Empire State Building. She and her sister Doris wrote *Disability Right Movement from Charity to Confrontation*.[12]
- The French journalist, Mr. Jean Do, had a massive heart attack that caused him to go into a coma for twenty days. He emerged from the coma with his entire body paralyzed. Only his left eyelid was moveable. Nevertheless with this compelling physical challenge, he did write and publish a book two days prior his death.[13]
- Chance Mair, who has Asperger's syndrome, started school in a special education classroom but graduated as valedictorian.[14]

---

[11] "Ron Whyte, 47, Dead; Playwright of Disabled," *New York Times*, September 19, 1989, www.nytimes/1989/09/19/obituaries/ron-whyte-47-dead-playwright-of-disabled.html.

[12] www.temple.edu/tempress/authors/zames_memoriam2.html.

[13] Kar Yee Katherine Law, 3 (2011)(03):1–2.

[14] Steve Ringman, "Teen with Asperger's Goes from Special Ed to Valedictorian," *The Seattle Times*, June 10, 2015.

This arbitrary list, taken from a sea of the CP, manifests what there is to be harnessed with the help of a supportive educational system. Their invaluable contributions, sparked by their own ailments or loved ones, continue to reposition and give the CP a more positive image to the public.

Chapter 5

Experiences in the Day Programs and Jobs for the Challenged Population

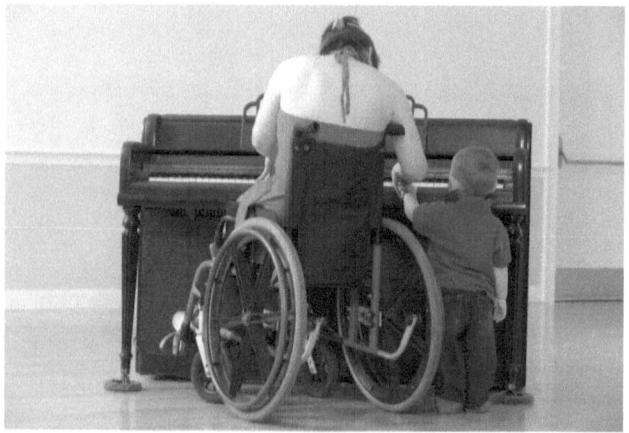

"A disabled mum along with her kid"

A normal day in the employment center unfolds like this. By eight in the morning, some staff arrive at the center, preparing the place for the day's activities. Thirty minutes later the vehicles start arriving with the consumers, and over time the arrival pattern becomes relatively fixed. The vehicles start arriving like ships at the dock. Around nine fifteen we have the peak moment, where one could see an average of three vehicles all lined up, waiting to drop off their passengers.

The comradeship among the bus drivers, aides, consumers, and staff is vividly depicted at the scene. Most consumers alight and are taken to their respective units. But we have a few consumers who sometimes make it very challenging for their drivers, aides/conductors, and staff alike to get them out of the vehicles.

Immediately they are settled in their respective units and become engaged with their contract work. This work, which involves making cardboard boxes and filling each with a sponge, is used to package hearing aids for a manufacturing company. The agency of the center pays the consumers for doing this job. Interestingly the consumers know this is their workplace and treat it as such. One particular consumer from Iron Hill Group Home is a workaholic and practically works throughout the day.

By midday they are ready for their lunch break. A few consumers help with the lunch preparation. Theo, a consumer, diligently works with Josephine, our chef lady. Incidentally 90 percent of our consumers are assisted with their lunches. Some have their food pureed; others have their chopped. And most have Thick-it added to their liquids to aid in swallowing. A few can feed themselves, and that similar percentage requires special feeding by the nurses. In all cases these consumers do their best to enjoy their lunches. The comradeship expressed in the lunchroom is awesome.

Every individual's birthday is celebrated, similar to Applebee's. At lunchtime, if a consumer and/or staff has a birthday, one staff member will make the announcement. Then staff, together with other consumers, will sing the birthday song, and lighthearted jokes can be heard in the lunchroom. After having their lunch, consumers are changed and then ready for the afternoon session.

Each unit has a particular main activity they are known for. In unit one, the movie room, consumers watch movies either owned by the center or brought in by staff or consumers. Unit two is the music and games room. Again staff creativity adds more spice to these units. In this particular unit a varied form of activities are carried out. Madam Quinn, having a wealth of experience in these matters only rivaled by her empathy for the consumers, engages them very much.

First, despite their challenges, these consumers are encouraged to participate in current affairs. Staff brings in current newspapers, magazines, and journals from which weather reports, sports, and political and domestic issues are shared. Horoscopes are read relating to each consumer, and games of interest are played. Some of these games include Family Feud, cards, bingo, and Chinese checkers. Also, interesting quotes, quizzes, and short stories are read to consumers.

In all of these activities, a great sense of belonging and accomplishment is felt from the consumer's participation. Interestingly only a few of these consumers are verbal. The others communicate through their boards, and with keen listening to sounds uttered by them, coupled with their body language, much is communicated. These seeming impediments are surmounted by the sheer determination of the consumers to live their lives to the fullest.

It is logical to say Madam Quinn's unit naturally attracts quite a percentage of the consumers. The other units also do their part in engaging the consumers to meet their needs. Some continue with contract work and/or watch special sitcoms or favorite Western movies.

In addition, the center caters for special activities such as yoga classes and prayer sessions that take place on a weekly basis. By two thirty the consumers start leaving for their respective residences. 80 percent of these consumers come from the agency's homes, while the remaining 20 percent come from other agencies or family homes. The percentage of the latter is growing as consumers continue to appreciate working at these centers.

A few years ago in Hills Field Center, a set of consumers were very competitive when it came to their contract work. Joe Park always strove to outdo Johnny and Daniel. Considering staff has to assist them in completing their tasks, much tact has to be applied to ensure fair work assistance is given. All the same one could see the thrill in either's face when he realizes he did outdo the others. With other consumers they are satisfied to hear the amount of boxes they were able to complete.

Martha, now deceased, was one of the few consumers who could complete all the tasks, and she was quite a diligent worker. Also, a consumer named Alice could only work with her feet. This was quite an amazing sight to see her put the foam in the boxes and close them. Indeed we have learned or seen people do great feats with their lower limbs in absence of their hands. To witness this feat accomplished by one of the consumers gives them a big plus.

Indeed a great number of these consumers require staff assistance. The whole concept of working in these employment centers is not to view consumers as workers with the highest productivity level. Rather the sole aim is to engage our consumers to participate in a work process, thus seeing them as actively contributing to a production process. For some, being able to close the boxes is acceptable, while others placing the sponges in the boxes is good enough.

At the end of their morning work, the amount of boxes made is divided by the number of consumers who participated. Hence their paycheck for the two weeks is calculated. They, like the rest of the agency workforce, look forward to their paychecks.

At this point it is important to know how much inroad has been made toward making the labor force of the CP getting into the established population. In 1945 Congress enacted a law declaring the first week of October as the National Employment Physical Handicap Week. In 1968 this was expanded to the whole month of October. Eventually there came National Disability Employment Awareness Month (NDEAM).

Having worked in other centers, I see why the Hills Field Center is preferred. Unlike other agency centers being located in the vicinity of their main offices, this employment center is not. Its accommodation is quite spacious, though it hasn't lost the warmth that makes consumers feel cared for. Also, though other programs demonstrate, this employment center portrays a lot of collages. Precisely this is the hallmark of the Hills Fields Center, and Madam Quinn does hold her share. The walls of unit two, her workplace, are decorated with many collages telling the story of the consumers who work there. Also more pronounced is the current season, which Madam Quinn, through her innovativeness with artwork, does great justice to inform consumers and everyone of what it brings. All the four seasons are well depicted.

Nurses in the day programs are very professional, and if there is one employment center that truly follows Danielle's Law, Hills Fields Center is the one. A center with more than thirty consumers does have incidents, so it is not uncommon when this happens. When they do, to ensure optimum care and service is given, external assistance, as deemed fitting, is applied. Consumers prescribed for midday medications have theirs professionally administered. Also, a high degree of consumer care is received, and staff, nurses, and managers properly address every concern.

For a workplace to have a lot of cultural diversity, genders, and spectrum of ages ranging from twenties to seventies, it brings in several adjustments. This is necessary to embrace harmony and efficiency in the work center. Generally speaking, we all have our job description, which we try to execute. However, by our inherent behavior, not ill motivated, staff enthusiasm gets in the way. Some individuals have strict work ethics, accommodating zero tolerance for mistakes. Others, staff and consumers alike, bring in emotional issues to the workplace, creating more challenging situations. However, these incidents seldom happen, and when they do, they are professionally addressed.

Hills Field Center has quite a mixture of staff and consumers. Ms. Phi likes presenting herself as a top shelf executive, and though with good intentions to help our consumers, some staff misconstrue her as bossy. With hands akimbo, she is ready to jump enthusiastically into any seeming emergency. Madam Ruthy, a quite hardworking lady, has a slim frame with an incredible force that could surprisingly almost single-handedly assist our adorable 350-pound D. D.

Interestingly we do have our charismatic Staff Agnes, whom I usually dub the permanent substitute, and she constantly brings a spark of sunshine to both staff and consumers. Lest I forgot, the man of the moment, Joe, has an incredible energy to work that's only matched by his desire to talk. Nevertheless, just as his energy positively helps the center, so does his unending talk amuse both staff and consumers.

The rest of the workforce in Hills Field Center—Abdulai, Haminatu, Susan, Donna, and John—prefer to do their work with minimal drama. Despite all this array of characters, incidents happen, and when they do, they are professionally addressed. With Madam Foster, a very cool, demure manager; Sylvia, the meticulous head nurse; and Patrick, the energetic male nurse, it becomes very understandable why a stream of parents of our challenged community keep visiting the center.

Feeding, assisting with personal hygiene to teaching and generally enabling the consumers in making choices are carried out with a profound sense of empathy and sensitivity. For the ordinary individual, these tasks are performed on automatic response or with minimal consideration. However, with our individuals served, both physical and emotional considerations are at work. Ensuring that consumers at these moments feel relaxed is a fundamental factor in the equation.

When I was hospitalized for a few months with a broken femur, some of this personal assistance had to be given to me. This experience will definitely give one an understanding of what our challenged individuals undergo on a daily basis for their entire lifetimes.

From the above picture portrayed, each or most of the readership will understand why the CP deserves to be integrated in our communities and people should be willing to support them. At Hills Field Center, we do our best to create this climate. It is their workplace, so we should treat them as coworkers. Like in most workplaces, we will fully enjoy the comradeship and optimum productivity.

During the period I worked at these centers, a few consumers and staff passed away. The agency made it their obligation to have a repast for the bereaved. With regard to residential programs, bereavements of consumers receive similar responses. Relatives, staff, and friends of the bereaved do demonstrate their grief. For staff they have a long-term and close association with the deceased consumers. Thus after the burial, a day is chosen to have a memorial service at the day program.

The pastor presiding over the ceremony usually asks consumers to give tribute to their bereaved. In all of the occasions, one could hear the touching tributes uttered by these consumers. They truly express their empathy in a very unique way for their mates or staff. Recalling the memorial service of Raymond White, Doris Davies, commonly called D. D., reminded the house of how she missed Raymond singing "Obama, Obama" and how he would come to her unit, asking staff to make boxes. Jonathan of Iron Hill Group Hill, where Raymond last lived, remembered Ray for his smiles and saying, "I am not a boy; I am a man." These simple utterings resonated well with individuals attending the memorial service.

Other consumers of blessed memories were Catherine, Kelvin, and Kline. In the case of the latter, Kline of Iron Hill Group Hill, I could remember that fateful day. I was about to punch out and leave for the day when the employment manager asked if I could assist him. His Iron Hill Group Hill staff would be coming, and being the only male staff at the center then, I decided to stay. The following day I was shocked to learn that Kline had passed away. My consolation was being there and deferring other personal concerns that needed to be addressed.

Oftentimes staff had to escort consumers to the emergency unit at odd times. Substitutes and regular staff have to forgo their personal appointments to meet these calls, hoping the residential staff of the consumers in question would relieve them. Sometimes for whatever reasons, this is not the case. However, one does feel gratified believing the choice made was the right one.

Given the above incidents, one sees a holistic picture of what transpires in our day programs, and as management gives a conducted tour to the prospective consumer with his or her guardian, these instances sometimes flash in our minds. Again some staff members, Madam Quinn, for one, believe these day programs could be rearranged to better serve the consumers. From an infrastructure standpoint, the facility could be customized to meet consumers' needs. Precisely the restrooms could have better clearance, and the Hoyer lift could be made a standard for both day programs, as it is in most residential homes.

Recently due to incidents that occurred in the restroom, certain shelves were removed to create better clearance. Also, Madam Quinn's workplace, unit two, now has a flat-screen TV, which will be used for afternoon recreational events. This strongly indicates that, with constant effort in advocating for the CP, positive response will continue to emerge.

Here is a conversation held in unit two in Hills Field Center among Haminatu, Madam Quinn, and Ruthy, all staff members.

Walking into unit two, Haminatu saw Madam Quinn and Ruthy engaged with the guys. "Whoa! I see you have a full house. Seems you're taking most of our guys."

Madam Quinn briefly paused from her reading to the group and replied, "Not really. I just like engaging these guys as much as possible. You will be amazed with how much they can do."

Ruthy, who was almost finished packing the contract boxes with Jim, one of our consumers, looked toward Haminatu and responded, "Guess you need my assistance."

"Actually, we need help with Lizi. You know Agnes did not work today," Haminatu replied.

Ruthy, despite her relatively small frame, single-handedly assisted D. D. and Mary, two of the center's heavyset ladies. "Well, give me a few minutes, and I will join you guys in the changing room."

At this point Pricilla came in to move D. D. out of unit two to her room in unit three. In her peculiar voice, D. D. asked Miss Pricilla, "How many boxes did I make this morning? Guess sixty."

Pricilla said, "I believe you made about forty, but we will double-check when we get to the room."

At this point Madam Quinn was in full steam with her group, getting positive answers of what they knew about New Jersey local news.

About the program itself, radicalization of the present system has been discussed. One person with that mind-set is Madam Quinn. There's simply a need for the DSPs to have rich job content and be actively involved in the process of amending and providing services to the consumers, all to provide better service to the consumers.

Basically these consumers started attending schools with special needs, and upon graduation, they do come to these day programs. Hence services here should not be focused as just work centers with some recreational amenities. Rather the establishment or agency should incorporate provisions that will continue to sustain and develop talent or abilities still latent within the consumers. The program should be designed to allow DSPs to work with consumers and create levels of assistance. Presently day programs address these issues with a specialized workforce that intermittently work with staff and consumers.

Here in New Jersey, most agencies have their residential group homes along with their day programs, for example, ARC of Middlesex, Somerset, Union, and most ARCs for that matter. Some also have schools that cooperate with these settings, for example, the Allegro School, which serves students ages three to twenty-one years old from ten counties in northern and central New Jersey.

Also, the Durand Academy and community service special education school have an adult training service that assists this population with prevocational training as well as independent living skills. Again, a few combine these services with special health and job placement—for example, Matheny School and Hospital and Midland Adult Services.

The latter render services in the transition of the consumers from school to adult life. They successfully carry out job training and placement for these youths.

Job Placement

This is the service some provider agencies have collaborated strongly with other national agencies to ensure the CP has significant employment in our communities. Cerebral Palsy Association of Middlesex County is one example of a service provider that meets these needs. It runs the Lakeview School and operates in twenty-five locations throughout the States.

Source America is a national leader in creating jobs from a skilled and dedicated workforce, people with significant disabilities.[15] This entity, which was established over forty years ago, was briefly known as National Industry for the Severely Handicapped (NISH). It also became part of Ability One, precisely one of two agencies established to assist with the implementation of the Federal Ability One Program. It is estimated that the United States has more than ten million working age people with significant disabilities who do not have jobs. Source America is working very hard to give these people employment.

Amazing Stories

In addition to the Americans with Disabilities Act (ADA), Senator Tom Hawkins (D-IA) made further efforts at the Senate, who moved the United Nations treaty on the Convention of the Rights of Persons with Disabilities (CRPD). Of the 196 United Nation member nations, 150 of them ratified CPRD. The United States, the first country in the world to adopt legislation banning discrimination against people with disabilities, is one of the few nations yet to ratify the treaty.[16]

Interestingly, as the legislative arm is working tirelessly to empower our disabled community so individuals from this challenged community continue to demonstrate their resilience. For example:

- Tim Harris, who has Down syndrome, dreamed to become a restaurant owner. He eventually became the proud owner

---

[15] www.sourceamerica.org/customers/federal-government.
[16] A speech by John Kelly.

of Tim's Place in Albuquerque, New Mexico. This story was featured on CBS, NBC, ABC, CNN, NPR, and *The View*.[17]

- Matt Cottle, who is autistic, dreamed to be a baker. He lived his dream to become owner of Stuttering King Bakery.
- Fernando Coruja, proprietor of Eva's Mexican food restaurant in Arizona, though not disabled, dreamed of uniting people into a common core by empowering their abilities. He helped thirty persons with disabilities achieve their dreams of employment.

In all these examples, employment was created for the disabled persons.[18]

The list of men, women, and entities that have made incredible contributions to ensure the CP has their fair share of employment in the American workforce is indeed a long one. These individuals have bravely challenged supposedly insurmountable circumstances to ensure their noble dreams become a reality. Valiant employees in Ability One alone will produce inspiring stories for this cause.

For those not mentioned, the simple reason is brevity. I greatly commend your selfless effort in creating employment for the CP.

Returning to the day programs, one sees how much is done to ensure our CP becomes gainfully employed. In these settings volunteers do come to the day centers to help with the program activities. The volunteers come from institutions of higher learning or in large groups. In either case the consumers do welcome these visits, and much fun and knowledge is incorporated in these exercises. All parties do gain from these visits.

---

[17] www.SourceAmerica.org/images/attachment/workplan.

[18] These wonderful stories were paraphrased from a speech given by E. Robert Chamberlin, president of Source America (www.SourceAmerica. org/images/attachment/workplan).

Chapter 6

The Support Systems of the Challenged Population

The support systems of this CP do play an integral part in ensuring the population's sustainability and growth. Generally speaking these groups assist the consumer to make choices and live a better life. Previously much has been said about the parent or guardian, the DSPs, and the primary medical care given by the nurses.

Here much attention will be focused on the administrative staff that ensures the agency is well structured to give quality care to its consumers. Then the medical team fully addresses consumers' health concerns. Also, educational entities within the agency and outside institutions provide the much-needed training facility that ensures standards are met and growth is assured in this field. Further, the technical support entity gives maintenance service, including research to make breakthroughs in technical accessories, adaptive equipment, and other devices for the consumers. Finally, the government regulatory arm, DHS, consolidates the entire support system and empowers development in the CP.

The administration of most agencies servicing the CP is similarly structured. Some departments like finance and infrastructural maintenance departments do not directly interact with the consumers like human resources, residential, and employment services do. But they do give needed services to ensure the smooth running of the agency.

1) <u>*Graphic illustration of the support systems of an Agency.*</u>

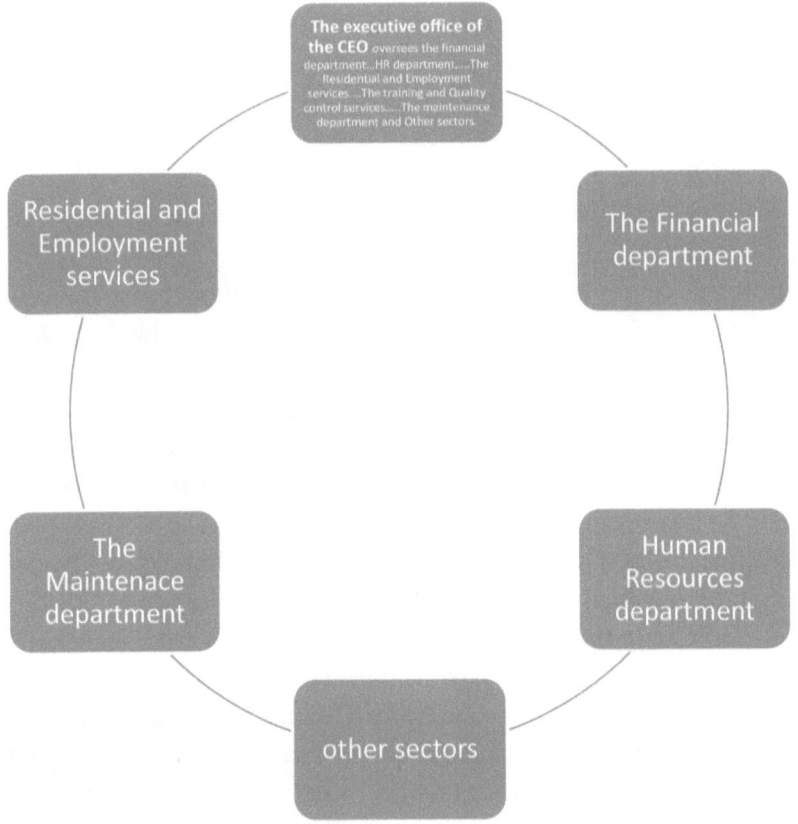

Staff initially interacts with the office from their employment phase. Then training sessions later come to address complaints or receive benefits. Apart from agencies' annual parties, forums have been created to bridge the void that sometimes exists between office staff and those in the field. Some agencies have wellness programs, company open houses, agency weeks, and other social interactive programs. This continuously created, amicable climate helps both parties to lend quality care to the consumers, our primary concern.

Some agencies have specialists who periodically visit the group homes and employment centers to ensure the developed plans are carried out. This emanates from the consumers' Individual Habitation Plan (IHP), behavioral plan, individual developmental plan, or other related plans. The advent of computerization has greatly helped to communicate this information to all parties concerned. Therap has made significant input in this regard. With Therap, communication in the agency has greatly improved, thus making it on a need-to-know basis. Information is efficiently disseminated in the establishment. Members within the agency conduct a greater percentage of their work through Therap. Apart from enhancing the paperless trend, professionalism, tracking, and a quick overview on subjects of interest are readily available.

Some agencies use their Intranet and e-mail networks through which most official communication is done. Also, the agency websites greatly support this communication process. This method of communication, despite the training sessions given to staff, has not gone without incidents. On a few occasions, staff has used this platform to challenge their peers' views unprofessionally, hence derailing the process. However, with the training process in place, this situation is on the decline.

DSPs are advocating that the specialized roles usually performed in a periodic time frame be in cooperation with those of the DSPs, hence creating levels of DSP, a trend that is presently pursued to become licensed professionals and give the necessary accreditation to this field.

In addition to the nurses who do give core support to the consumers, the health care services ensure consumers have strong ancillary support through their medical insurance. This includes the services of the rehabilitation entities when required. In essence, access to hospitals, medical specialists, and all needed health personnel is made available. This vital arm ensures the consumers utilize their health to the fullest. Their medical, dental, and all other associated appointments are followed through.

Along with the many interventions made in this population, specifically with the adaptive products, some companies, for example, Invacare and DynaVox, ensure Medicaid do assist in procuring their devices if this population needs them.[19] Invacare is notably the world's leading manufacturer of wheelchairs, scooters, respiratory products, and other home care products.[20]

---

[19] www.dynavoxtech.com/funding/medicaid.

[20] www.invacare.com/cgi-bin/imhqprd/default; www.medicarecode.net/tag/invacare/.

The training unit within the agency ensures that its workforce receives current and standard training programs, as the DDD mandates. For most agencies, emphasis is placed on DDD-mandated training programs. After the new recruits have successfully passed these trainings, the agency work can commence. In most cases each agency training program is tailored to the type of consumers they service.

Generally some agencies do restrain their consumers, hence having spar trainings. Others have physically challenged consumers, so subjects like wheelchair training and lifting carry high priority. In all agencies these trainings are completed annually or after every two years. Also, most agencies relate to institutions that provide necessary (pertinent) trainings for their staff. In addition, they encourage staff to improve their education specifically in the field or otherwise.

The Elizabeth Boggs Center is an educational institution, precisely a university center for excellence in developmental disabilities. This center values uniqueness and significantly contributes to training and pursuing further knowledge to the CP. Elizabeth Boggs founded the center in 1983 for the sole purpose of, as defined, "This center provides community and student training, and technical assistance, conduct research and model demonstrations disseminates educational materials and respond to request for information."[21] The center has gradually progressed to researching knowledge that will be used on persons with physical and mental disabilities. The center supports collaboration, community training, and technical assistance and disseminates information and educational materials.[22]

The Somerset County Transportation for Freeholders is one of the organized transportation systems that help move the CP around. In addition, agencies have their fleet of vehicles, along with other entities and parents of the CP. The DHS has carried out some work stipulating what fixtures should be housed in the vehicles to mandatory training that the transporters should take.

Several incidents over the years have precipitated the use of specific means of securing our consumers to ensure their safety. Also, the Department of Transportation, in conjunction with DHS, has enacted specific safety laws. The Americans with Disabilities Act (ADA) of 1990

---

[21] http://rwjms.umdnj.edu/boggscenter.

[22] Elizabeth Boggs Center's certificate they give through Rutgers University.

prohibits discrimination and ensures equal opportunity and access for persons with disabilities. This includes special identification cards and registration plates for parking privileges.[23]

The technical arm that services this CP has improved greatly from the manufacturing of simple wheelchairs to making motorized wheelchairs, having nonverbal consumers use their customized boards, and building very sophisticated computerized screens to meet the consumers' needs. Also on the list are protective headgear, tableware, and other adaptive items. Prosthetics and braces for the limbs and neck are also part of the devices that have been greatly improved on for the CP. Very renowned manufacturing companies in the field have produced lifting devices of all types, namely vehicle, porch, and rail lifts.[24] A few of these are Freedom Lift System and Bruno.

The technical arm also ensures that the consumers enjoy high-quality maintenance service of their products. One specific example is the work done by the sporting companies, particularly wheelchairs for extreme sports, that have been in existence since 1986. George Murray and Chris Peterson have been affiliated with Invacare in Elyria, Ohio, the world's leading manufacturer and distributor of medical products. Other examples are the nonacute equipment, which are of popular use by the CP and particularly the physically challenged population. Just like the medical sector enthusiastically researches autism for quick interventions, so does the technical arm envision how their product will be of maximum use to the consumers.

Matheny Medical and Educational Center is primarily a special hospital and educational facility for children and adults with medical and complex disabilities.[25] From their website, it is learned that, among other work conducted by the center, they research developmental disabilities in such areas as medicine, cognition rehabilitation technology, occupational therapy, and audiology. Also, the center has successfully

---

[23] For more-comprehensive information, visit www.fta.dot.gov/civil rights/12345.html. Here, the U.S. Department of Transportation and Federal Transit Administration (FTA) talks about the ADA Act of 1990. Furthermore, in part 27, volume 80, of the *Federal Register*, the rules of regulation, as recent as March 2015, are stated.

[24] See references at the back.

[25] www.matheny.org.

worked on studies for the use of nonverbal patient stimulators in the training of medical students to work effectively with persons who have developmental disabilities. The long list of research continues with studies of cognition in persons with neurodevelopmental disorders.

Also important—this center plays a key role in facilitating collaboration among faculty from medical schools and schools in allied field work related to developmental disabilities. Their maintenance division greatly helps with wheelchairs and some adaptive equipment used by the consumers. They have incorporated a maintenance mobile van called "workshop on wheels" that helps in carrying out their maintenance work. Also, a list of medical equipment stores in New Jersey render this service in addition to sales of this adaptive equipment. They usually work with Medicaid in the purchase of these items required by the consumers.

Fortunately, Matheny Center has secured a significant place regarding their association with the CP. Their medical contribution, actually interventions, has been quite impactful to the CP. They have a strong collaboration with the University of Medicine and Dentistry of New Jersey (UMDNJ). They have pediatricians who have carried out successful projects on the CP.[26]

Matheny Medical and Educational Center has a preschool through twelfth grade for ages three to twenty-one. The teachers are fully certified in special education and highly qualified to teach core curriculum content areas.

Individual with Disability Educational Act (IDEA) and Section 504, the Rehabilitation Act of 1973 that protects qualified individuals from discrimination based on their disabilities, do empower the CP regarding their educational goals. The above institutions clearly complement these efforts of educating the CP and further continue to train members of their support system.

At the Hills Field Center, our consumers use quite a number of wheelchairs, with some manual and others motorized. The consumer's wheelchair is an extension of his or her physical being. With keen observation, you can particularly tell the manner they handle these wheelchairs. They relax, work, and fight with them if they have to. However, staff ensures the last option is always avoided.

---

[26] See www.disabilityhealth.org.

Though a few consumers have electronic boards mounted on their wheelchairs, they hardly use these devices. The consumers prefer using their communication boards to converse with staff or people in general. David of Iron Hill Group Home loves using his manual wheelchair and converses very much with his communication board. His ability to use these devices extremely well is clearly seen by his participation in his unit, the long telephone conversations, and, of course, his executive positions in the many groups he belongs to. In his self-advocacy group, he was their whip, and he has represented his peers several times in DDD programs.

Despite the challenge to communicate, David, with endless resilience, will ensure that he communicates. One morning he came to me, pointing to his board to inform me about something very important. Initially I thought he wanted to do his morning contract work, but I was wrong. He decided to take the bull by the horn and led me to the closet in the unit. Getting his hint, I paid full attention to his board, and I realized what he was communicating to me. It was very sensitive of him. A sympathy card had been bought for Andrew, one of the drivers. Since Andrew had just arrived and Madam Quinn was not at work, he wanted the card to be delivered to Andrew to express their sympathy for Andrew's brother who had passed away. You could see how happy he was when I placed the card on his communication board to deliver it to Andrew.

Finally, in this category of supporting systems is DDD, which is part of DHS. They ensure that all these supporting systems do adhere to the standards established by them. These standards sincerely help to make sure the consumers have good choices. To bring a clearer overview, DHS does coordinate its effort of assisting our CP by working with other arms of the executive. These are mainly the Departments of Health, Justice, Labor, Transportation, Education, Treasury, and Housing and Urban Development. Again, I am just delving into the periphery of DDD scope of work, for the state of New Jersey entails much.[27]

Since 1959, DDD has provided funding for more than 280 agencies in communities throughout the state. They presently have six developmental centers in six counties, namely Somerset, Hunterdon, Burlington, Cumberland, Cape May, and Middlesex. Furthermore,

---

[27] www.state.nj.us/humanservices/ddd/home.

they work with the Supportive National Housing Program, from which there is Special Needs Housing Partnership Loan Program (SNHPLP), which is aimed at creating affordable, supportive housing for people with developmental disabilities.[28] This program, launched in June 2013, is a special needs housing partnership, creating affordable housing for six hundred people with developmental disabilities. This will help to integrate people with special needs into the community.[29]

Again, we have either support from the consumers' direct self-advocacy or vibrant advocacy from agencies like Easter Seals, as it has been with the CP for more than sixty-five years.[30] Also, we have American Association on Intellectual and Developmental Disabilities (AAIDD), which seeks to strengthen the capacity of professionals in the CP and participate in the development of a fully inclusive society.[31]

Advocating for the CP continues to gain solid footing.[32] The consumers do their advocacy from attending house meetings to representing on boards where their participation is essential. Though their representation will not be that of the brightest advocates, the effect of concerns emanating from them resonate well with the authorities, the government in particular. Also, at times when the government might believe it is justified in reducing the CP budgets, as stated below, there is a strong case to counter these actions.

An article by Claude Brodesser-Akner, New Jersey Advance Media for NJ.com, states that Governor Chris Christie will promote community services but not back off from the plan to return some five hundred disabled people from out-of-reach state institutions. Also, from an article published in the *Seattle Times* on September 23, 2014, Joseph O. Sullivan states that a budget reduction will affect thousands of disabled people currently receiving state aid.

---

[28] www.state.nj.us/dca/hmfa/developers/needs/partnership.

[29] Contact Yirgu Wolde, Division of Supported Housing and Special Needs, (609) 278-7521.

[30] www.easterseals.com/NJ.

[31] www.aaiddjournals.org.

[32] Reference the 2013 book by Janet Sauer, *Negotiating the Social Borderlands: Portraits of Young People with Disabilities and Their Struggles for Positive Relationship.*

The above groups put up very successful fights. The participation of agencies like Easter Seals and other advocacy networks has led to many positive changes enacted by DDD. A current issue is the Medicare physician payment formula. On April 14, 2015, the Senate passed the Medicare Access and Children's Health Insurance Plan (CHIP) Reauthorization Act of 2015 by a vote of ninety-two to eight.

Included in the list of advocacy organization is Action DD.[33] This body licensed in the state of Washington advocates for people with developmental disabilities, all without government money.

Thus the very exercise of making the universal population come to embrace the CP is very effectively done by DDD. True agencies have promoted the positive image of the consumers through their websites, and independent bodies have effectively used press conferences, letters, journals, rallies, and phone calls to reinforce and drive home this awareness. However, the government arm has solidified the change by lending legal strength so the general populace will accept the CP.

The above has brought about meaningful changes like changing "handicapped" to "disabled," as the former connoted a negative meaning. Even the word "consumer" is gradually fading out to be replaced with "challenged individuals" and "intellectually served." When fiscal issues adversely affect the CP, institutions have strongly advocated on behalf of the CP. And DDD has come in very supportive. The present establishment of the central registry of offenders against individuals with developmental disability reaffirms this meaningful change.[34]

Tertiary institutions[35] are working very aggressively to come out with breakthrough results that will address issues of autism, Down syndrome, bipolar, brain injuries, and attention-deficit/hyperactivity disorder (ADHD) prevalent in the CP. These interventions carried out in the early stages will be very beneficial to this population.

Brain Balance Achievement Center is located at Princeton. The bulk of these centers are on the East Coast, but they are generally franchise establishments all over the States. Founded by Dr. Robert Melilo and

---

[33] www.actionaa.com.

[34] This law had bipartisan support and was signed into action by Governor Chris Christie on April 30, 2010.

[35] You can research specific journals that authenticate these claims.

established with William Fowler, they specifically help children with ADHD.[36]

Also, studies are progressively carried out to establish DSPs as having a professional body status. This process, when successfully carried out, will be a landmark in this field. Specifically Elizabeth Boggs Center, University of Medicine and Dentistry of New Jersey, merged with Rutgers University in 2013, forming a new Rutgers School of Biomedical and Health Sciences.

In addition, Elizabeth Boggs did collaborative work, stating dates when DSP certificates were given. The Boggs Center inception in 1983 is part of UMDNJ. Furthermore, activities of the Boggs Center are guided by the consumer advisory council and partnerships with people with disabilities, families, state and community agencies, and policymakers.

The magazine for wheelchair sports and recreation by Jeff Odorm gives insight on the disabled community participation in recreational activities. Some of the products made are wheelchairs—everyday, basketball, tennis, and racing. Disabled Sport USA is a website that gives information on sports accomplishments by the disabled population. "Since 1967, Disabled Sports USA has focused on one goal: to improve the lives of wounded warriors, youth and adults with disabilities by providing sports and recreation opportunities."[37]

Invacare Medicaid.gov provides health coverage to over 8.8 million nonelderly individuals with disabilities, including those who are working and those who want to work. A federal statute provides for both mandatory and optional coverage for individuals with disabilities.

Another company that contributed through technical intervention toward bettering the lives of our CP is DynaVox. For over twenty-five years, they have developed technology through clinical research and customer feedback, helping thousands of individuals with limited or no speech due to a variety of causes including stroke, autism, cerebral palsy, amyotrophic lateral sclerosis (ALS), or traumatic injury.

This company grew from a trio. Greg Lillian and Professor Mark Friedman teamed with Tilden Bennett form Sentient System Technology in 1983. Their product, the Eye Typer, brought a gift of communication

---

[36] www.brainbalancecenters.com.
[37] www.disabledsportsusa.org/about-us/our-story.

to the millions of Americans unable to speak due to cerebral palsy, autism, and so forth. They grew with this one revolutionary communication product to now employing more than 350 people worldwide and being the world-leading provider of communication and education solutions for individuals with speech, language, and learning disabilities.[38]

To ensure the CP has maximum benefit from these technological interventions, DynaVox and Mayer-Johnson have incorporated the funding of Medicare and state medical assistance for their products.[39]

Sometimes receipt for Supplemental Security Income (SSI) does not guarantee eligibility for Medicaid. Also, Medicaid and Children Health Insurance Program (CHIP) provide institutional settings and health-care benefit resources known as a delivery system.

It is believed the above support system will give the readership more understanding of how these entities relate to the CP. Each entity plays a role that truly enables the individually challenged to live a better life in the community.

---

[38] wwwdynavoxtech.com/community.
[39] Visit funding@dynavoxtech.com.

Chapter 7

Special Inputs

There are times when things move out of the normal to challenged situations we refer to as emergencies. Here in the CP, we do encounter these situations; hence provisions are put in place to accommodate them. The famous Danielle's Law simply states that, whenever staff believes the consumer's life is in danger, 911 should be called. Failing to do this will attract a $5,000 fine for first offenders and then $10,000 and subsequently $25,000 for repeated offenses. Also, most agencies have a protocol to follow when incidents occur in the residential homes or employment centers to ensure consumers are cared for and incidents are properly documented.

At South Wood Group Home was Kennedy, an independent consumer who loved faking seizures to ensure the nurses stationed in the hospital treated him. The high frequencies of his alleged seizures became a serious concern. This appalling situation caused a special meeting to be convened to address the issue. First, the EMT team came to know about South Wood Group Home frequently calling 911. However, as a professional response service, they have to arrive. Also, the neurosurgeon, on frequent examination, confirmed Kennedy was having fake seizures. He advised for the paramedics to bring him only when his checklist confirmed he did have a seizure.

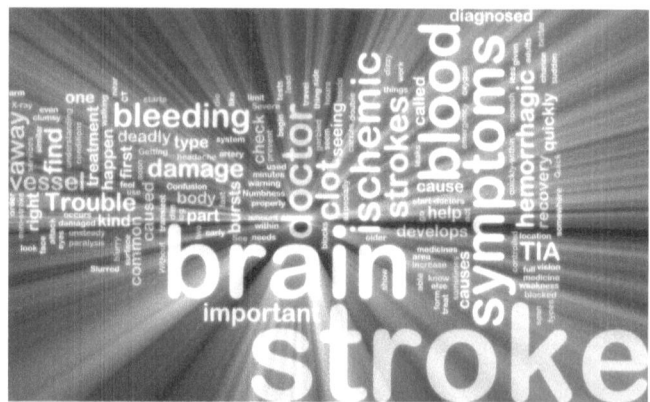

"Read some of our challenges"

One day Kennedy experienced a seizure, and the paramedics were called. He was taken to the hospital, but as soon as he was checked, he was discharged. The next day I took him to his primary physician for examination, and again he was certified as okay. Outside the doctor's office, Kennedy had another seizure there, and I had to call 911. Along with the paramedics came the cops. There the cops told me Kennedy was having a pseudo seizure, but considering the situation, we had to take him to the hospital, which was two minutes away.

Later I talked with Kennedy about his high frequency of seizures, and he candidly told me he liked to be treated by the nurses, much so when he realized the doctor's office where he happened to be was just a few minutes away from the hospital.

This is an indication of the ordeal that staff will have to go through.

Better Understanding of the Challenged Population by the Law Enforcers

In an article, "First to Respond: Sometimes the Last to Know", published in the *People and Families Journal*, the author Jonathan Jaffe clearly stated how members from the CP are often mistaken for other offenses. Specifically the motorist with cerebral palsy is mistaken for a drunken driver, the teenager with intellectual disabilities is disregarded as an unreliable witness, and the man with involuntary seizures is arrested for pushing a police officer.

Hence there is a dire need for law enforcement and first responders—namely police officers, firefighters, emergency medical technicians, judges, court bailiffs, and correction officers—to be more trained in understanding the individually challenged in our communities. As David Whelan, project director for first responders, rightly stated, "People with autism, Down syndrome and other disabilities have been harmed because of lack of training among first responders."[40]

It is reassuring to know that much effort is ongoing by New Jersey Crisis Intervention Training (CIT) in providing intensive training to identify and assist people with mental health issues and developmental disabilities who are in crisis. These initiatives will positively impact current fatal gun incidents. The primary participants in some of these incidents were labeled as mentally ill, along with the intellectually and developmentally challenged individuals.

Now it sometimes intrigues one why these behaviors happen to our guys. Yes, one will ask, "What an odd question!" However, despite the population one is dealing with, a few issues require serious research. Why do we have a steady increase of this population in this country as compared to other places?

Initially I thought the provision given to our consumers is a reflection of a country with great empathy for its challenged people. With other countries, such provision available to this population is not even there for their normal population. It's quite true. In other situations, having the capacity to fully identify this population and care for them is a daunting task. Hence only partial assistance is given.

Again as one continues with this discussion, some schools of thoughts suggest the food we consume here in this country is a factor. Compared to some countries where this CP is relatively low, their food intake is significantly different from what we have here in the United States. However, this submission requires a complete study in the future.

Another instance happened at North Brunswick Group Home. Martin, a resident, was having an increase in his behavioral issues. All was okay during the evening, and just after meds were administered at eight

---

[40] New Jersey Council on Developmental Disabilities (NJCDD), *Journal, People, and Families* (Winter 2015).

in the evening, an argument broke out between Martin and Charles. Staff had to quickly intervene to protect lives and property. However, though no bodily harm occurred, Martin's increase in behavioral situation demanded taking him to UMDNJ for assessment. By the time all formalities were addressed, which required Martin's stay at the unit, the time I left for home was three in the morning the next day.

At South Wood Group Home, an incident led to the dismissal of two overnight staff. As in most agencies, to ensure consumer care is maintained, administrators do drop-ins, that is, unannounced administrative checks. This particular night the two administrators came at two in the morning; however, after several knocks at the door, they decided to enter the home.

Both overnight staff were soundly asleep, even when the administrator went to check the house. They saw the dining table already set for breakfast and medication placed in their cups with the van keys on the table. The group home van was already backed up by the entrance, so in the morning, the entire routine would go on as clockwork. Unfortunately they did not anticipate the arrival of the administrators; hence disciplinary action was carried out.

Unlike the above, John, a staff member known for standing his ground, had a show when two administrators knocked at his group home around midnight. He answered them and demanded the reason for their visit. They explained it was a drop-in so he should let them in. He demanded their work identity. Without which, he would not allow them, because this would endanger the consumers and himself. Since they had no agency identification with them, they had to leave.

Many incidents occurred where normal shifts would be full of behavioral issues, hence leading to a lot of documentation in addition to the routine paperwork. However, this is what the job entails, and as RCs and caregivers in general, one must be ready.

Sometimes situations occur so quickly that it becomes very difficult to believe them. One Saturday morning a staff member with his consumer from the same agency came to visit our group home. Incidentally I had worked with this staff member several years back in another agency.

We reminisced about those years we used to work together. I had also recently assisted the consumer to the present apartment where he was living. In the discussion that transpired, I told him to put on his best behavior because that was one condition that qualified him to live in the apartment. Not long after they left for their home.

Less than an hour later, we were informed that these two individuals had a tragic accident a few blocks from our group home and were in the emergency ward. This news truly shocked us, considering these two people had been talking with us less than an hour ago.

One incident brought about a permanent change in one of our elderly consumers. Marcus of Mountain Group Home had been getting frailer and sleeping less at night. One morning my partner was about to assist him with his personal hygiene when he saw a significant discoloration around his left hip. A 911 call was made, and after preliminary examination by the emergency medical technician, he was taken to St. Peter's emergency ward. All protocols regarding documentation were carried out, and I had to escort him to the hospital.

At the emergency room, several tests were done, and eventually he was admitted to the hospital. As part of the final outcome, Marcus was discharged to a rehab facility, starting his final exit from his group home where he had lived a great part of his adult life.

Every caregiver will tell you similar stories of how a day on the job almost became a nightmare or simple incidents escalated to emergencies. A consumer named Mustapha had issues so he was temporarily housed in Reunion Group Home. One Saturday morning we were at work when the female staff told me Mustapha was attempting to leave the home.

By the time I arrived at the dining room, Mustapha was exiting through the backdoor. I tried to redirect him, but it was to no avail. Instead he headed for the neighbors' compound. Following him, I realized the neighbor had a bulldog, which made the situation more challenging. Fortunately we communicated with the neighbor, who helped us get Mustapha back to his group home.

As with most organizations, the general workforce has to wrestle with top management over policies that each party believes is not written to his or her best interests. For instance, certain agencies will accept staff receiving gifts from guardians while others will not support such practices. Personal time off (PTO) will be accrued on a biweekly basis for one agency; others will have a progressive accrual by years of service. Also, disposing of these PTOs by sale is done differently by the agencies. Some buy them at their full value while others propose half price or use it before you can't accrue any more. These variations seen among agencies also add to staff contention for more incentives. In these organizations, interestingly, the managers or supervisors, as other agencies call them, are usually caught up in the crossfire.

Another key issue is staffing, which has been constantly addressed, but there still needs work done to produce the desired result. The manager is essentially left to come in when there is no staff to fill the absent spot. The crux of the matter is that managers are not given sufficient latitude or empowerment to handle this issue. Generally we have the x and y workpeople in all workplaces; hence authorities restricting overtime should take cognizance of this work pattern.

There are many instances where work schedules do not go as stated because staff calls out for so many reasons. And with management-imposed restrictions, substitution becomes difficult. It is believed that, with an objective outlook, the issue will be amicably resolved.

Also, despite the fact that changes do complement growth in any organization, frequent changes may impede growth or create a feeling of instability. This is felt when agencies continuously have new auto insurance writers and health insurance companies and so forth make it difficult for employees to keep up with the transitions.

Sometimes individuals do have issues with their agency and oftentimes reconcile their differences. In other instances a group of employees see an organizational issue and professionally try to address it. Well-thought-out proposals are forwarded to management; unfortunately management will give convenient diplomatic responses to justify the status quo. It is believed, if management sought for a win-win situation, an objective dialogue would follow, which would culminate into a productive conclusion.

The above situation has caused this workforce to informally establish a work insurance strategy. They have at most three jobs: a full time, part time, and substitute one. Immediately when they sense insecurity with any of these jobs, they look for another one and do the necessary substitution. This arrangement has proved doable with the caregiving service industry.

Chapter 8

Job Transition of the Caregivers and Their Effect on the Challenged Population

Readers at this stage will agree that, for sustainable employment with the CP, the caregivers should have a high degree of empathy for their consumers. However, the realities are that enumeration and upward mobility in this workplace should be sustainable to maintain even the most ardent consumer fan.

Truly the organizations in these challenging economic times have made good on some of these conditions to keep the workforce satisfied. Regular biweekly paychecks and work benefits that include health insurance, paid leave, and requirements for employees' educational growth are present. Also, management makes provisions for personal gratification by means of giving awards and interactions among staff, consumers, and management.

The human resource departments come up with creative measures to sustain existing programs for consumers and RCs and create new ones. Specifically these educational programs are meant to better serve consumers and, in other cases, create better interaction within the workforce. We see this in employment centers and residential day programs. However, monitoring methods in tracking employees' work time and use of the agency's material resources seem to gain precedent over initiating incentives for the workforce to productively contribute to the agency's growth.

Again the rising inflationary trend has caused management to be stringent with overtime hours, a temporary respite for staff. Incidentally this initiates the need for the workforce to start finding ways to address these socioeconomic realities.

Indeed the professional status of this CP was constructively visited, and the concern to have a formally licensed and certified body emerged.

The need to have a DSP was pursued. The Elizabeth Boggs Center, in conjunction with Rutgers University and several agencies in New Jersey, participated in this program. Conventions followed, which showed progress made, and several individuals from agencies graduated to the existing levels. However, meaningful conclusions are still to be reached.

Also, much is yet to be learned about what state accreditation and national professional licensing has been given to this body. The financial benefit given formally to DSP graduates have been minimal; thus for such detailed course work, transition to other professional fields has become the norm. A very popular transition has been to the nursing field.

In Mountain Group Home, the staffing could be considered relatively stable. Interestingly the managerial position was changing on an annual basis for a few years. The staff positions hardly changed, and if this happened, staff left for relocation or retirement reasons.

Recently all this changed. In one year, there was a mass staff turnover. Interestingly they did not leave the company, but their job descriptions were altered. Two staff became nurses, one from the overnight position and the other from the evening shift. Also, another staff got a well-paid job at an air transportation company and decided to step down his hours of work.

This situation was a wake-up call for workers in this home. Staff, including managerial, rationalized in various ways. Some decided to opt for the existing managerial positions; others intensified their search for better-paying jobs outside the agency and, in certain cases, beyond the vocation. Others decided to enroll in the nursing profession or seek advanced education. The remaining few decided to hold on to their two jobs and call it a day.

Interestingly a few RCs in other group homes became nurses. Some gained employment in the agency while others found employment elsewhere. This is the case for other agencies, but the rate is now on the high side. In other instances, it is not just the nursing profession, but other marketing professions like accounting, computer science, counseling, and so forth.

The cause for the transition is not only dependent on employees developing themselves for better-paid positions. Caregivers do not see a clearly mapped-out upward mobility in the direct care service in the CP. The alternative structure that has been in existence is staff gaining employment in the specialized services, be it psychiatry, psychology, sociology, or other fields. Furthermore, staff continues to seek employment in secondary departments like finance, human services, legal department, education, maintenance, and so forth.

This CP indeed has progressed with a battery of professionals in giving quality service to our cherished consumers. This brings to mind impactful interventions regarding autism, cerebral palsy, and effective learning modules that have been developed recently. Matheny Medical and Educational Center, Elizabeth Boggs Center, and establishments like the Brain Balance Achievement Center could serve as very good examples. But more advancement is to be made in crafting a core body, possibly executed by DDD. This body will directly develop the progress of the professional service component of the CP from a holistic perspective.

Searching the work horizon for a befitting pay

Thus we see the workforce, much so the direct caregivers of the CP initially as a transitional entry job where one uses it as a leverage to opt for better job after enrolling.[41] It is stated that a medical assistant's annual income is $29,100, which includes the DSP as well, the least paid in a group where you have pharmacists earning $113,390, physical therapists making $78,270, registered nurses taking home $65,950, and licensed practical nurses earning $41,150. Fortunately since the

---

[41] Bureau of Labor Statistics (BLS) reports from 2010 to 2020.

qualitative benefits are indeed rewarding, to some employees, this brings some stability to this workplace.

Generally most jobs are rated by how much the services are paid for, as reflected above. Nevertheless people sometimes take up a job primarily for the love of the position, hence giving them a good basis to excel. But the jobs in the health-care industry and particularly this challenged vocation have pay rates that fall on the low side. This is one main reason for job transition, consequently affecting the quality of service highly needed in this field.

One clearly sees job transition in this workplace at the weekend shift positions where individuals enroll as part-time workers. They usually work the weekend shift and, from my observation, last for six months to a year. These new employees are usually high school and sometimes first-year graduate students, who, for many reasons, decide to work in this field. Again their field of study is quite relevant to this work field. Some have a bachelor's degree in the social sciences and have a good amount of compassion toward the consumers.

Usually enthusiastic, they exhibit the potential of having a great future in the field; however, with time, they gradually make their exits. Whatever the reasons for their departure, I believe, if the work field is charted to strongly depict an upward mobility that relates to their qualifications, many will prefer to stay. This job transition is also evident in the office work place, though to a lesser extent.

Parents/Guardians Making Home Visits with Their Challenged Loved Ones

With all fairness some parents and guardians do take their children for home visits, and the number of parents exercising this practice do increase during festive seasons. These home visits last on average for a day or two, and then our individually challenged guys return to their residence. I commend these parents doing these home visits and believe they sincerely experience what RCs have to work with on a daily basis.

The moms do lead the dads in taking their loved ones for home visits, and in certain cases both parents do perform this role. The first group (moms and dads), regardless of the festive period, comes every weekend to take their child for a home visit. Indeed we see our guys happily leaving to spend quality time with mom and/or dad. Again when the consumers return, we observe the parents bidding them farewell, as our guys express relaxed feelings in their homes.

Rick of Mountain Group Home, ambulatory but nonverbal, will hug staff and smiles as he leaves with his mom. Scotty of Roosevelt Group Home, on returning, will give staff the "one love" hand blow to show his happiness in coming back to his group home. In all instances parents/guardian engage staff in meaningful conversation before leaving.

The other group does make regular calls to the consumers, on average once a week. This includes siblings of consumers and members of the first group. Indeed the consumers also make calls to their parents or guardians.

Thus these parents, though wanting their children to have the best care available, will also have a fair understanding what caregiving is about. Indeed most do, as seen by the way they express their gratitude, even though most agency policy forbids their employees from receiving gifts from them. Again these parents, by advocating for better incentives and pay increase for the RCs, will help increase quality service in the industry.

In discussing with individuals who have transitioned from RC to LPN or RN, they have this as a realistic argument. After being in the field for a reasonable amount of time, the desire to serve the consumers better leads them to the nursing field. Furthermore, serving as nurses, they were able to use their RC experience to better relate to their patients. Incidentally these patients were not necessarily intellectually and developmentally disabled but include geriatric and critical care individuals.

Sheriff, a transitioned nurse, realizes that, by talking to his patients who need acute care, he was able to give them better care. Before he used to suction them; however, by closer association, they voluntarily carried out this exercise unaided and with less stress. Under this interaction bedridden patients were also able to assist with their bedside care, hence improving their acute care situation.

It will be said that measures are put in place to ensure standards are maintained for the caregiving workforce. This is true, but how much has been done to realistically attract a high-caliber workforce that will bring breakthrough changes in the CP? This type of workforce will definitely help our CP.

One incident happened several years ago in an agency I worked for. This agency had a brand-new human resources director who was ready to make changes in the department and agency as a whole. Strict measures were put in place, and the work polices were carried out to the letter with zero tolerances in certain cases. Employees were met with progressive disciplinary action leading to termination, and vacancies were on the increase. In one instance the human resources department advised managers who were exhibiting leniency to forward such personnel matters to them for execution.

Consequently vacancies became difficult to fill, and after six months of this work situation, the human resources director was relieved of her duties. True, other issues could have culminated for the above to occur; however, if an amicable and rewarding environment has been the primary focus, these outcomes would have been averted.

Interestingly the CP also exists in a challenged universal environment, that is, the real world. Here, people battle with socioeconomic situations, their emotional struggles, and resources, particularly good health and time, which are not always abundantly available. Hence, job transition will continue to occur as the workforce seeks a better share of these resources.

Here is a conversation that transpired among two old and two new staff—Agnes, Robert, Pricilla, and Sheriff—while they were having lunch.

Sheriff gave a questioning look to Agnes. "Agnes, could you confirm if our designation here is a RC or a residential specialist? I sometimes get mixed up with these designations."

Agnes said, "Well, Sheriff, sometimes you know they call us simply caregivers, and now they say we are direct support professionals, or DSPs."

"Well," said Sheriff, "maybe any of these names will apply with what I see we do. As I get more aquatinted with the work, I realize we do engaged in assistance with our consumers."

Agnes smiled. "Well, I do not want to get you more confused at this stage. You see, we give medications and literally do a lot of nursing work. So why not say we are nurses? We do counsel them, redirect them, and ensure they meet with their goals, so are we not their physical therapists? Also, do not forget we constantly advocate for them at home, work, and all places we go with them. We do documentation for every incident. Could you not say we are their attorneys? I do not want to continue with the list."

Sheriff shook his head. "I am now thinking they should give us a good salary because of these many caps we wear. Don't you think so?"

Pricilla, who was partially munching his food and barely listening now, became interested. "Guys, talking about salary, I used to be a corporate manager on Wall Street, but we all know what happened with the economy, so we make some adjustments, however challenging."

Agnes replied, "Well, Pricilla, I guess many people in this caregiving industry can contribute to your story." She looked directly toward Sheriff. "Maybe when they come to that realization, but for now let's get on with our lunch, and thank God I like working with this population." Agnes took some interest in her food.

Robert entered smiling and feeling very reassured as he placed his food on the table. "Hi, guys. I want to share some good news with you."

"Shoot!" said Agnes and Sheriff in a chorus.

"Well," said Robert, "do you know there is a new agency that is actively recruiting caregivers and offering very attractive salary and benefits?"

"I know you are kidding," replied Agnes, becoming more interested. "Give us the down low. Maybe one will place an application."

"Seriously I just went through the first interview," said Robert. "The interesting part is that you will be surprised to know how many of our colleagues have already made a run for this offer."

Sheriff was seated with his palm on his chin with a faraway look in his eyes.

Robert then came close to him and patted him on the back. "Young man, I assume you're thinking at this point, 'Might be. What am I doing here?' Not so, Sheriff."

"Actually," replied Sheriff, nodding his head, "I do like working with these consumers, but as they are challenged, so too we are financially limited, and that has to be addressed."

In a lighthearted manner, Agnes replied, "Well, guys, we should soon be thinking of owning our own agencies someday." She chuckled.

Robert looked at Sheriff. "This is food for thought. Then we might be able to help adjust many concerns we've gone through."

They all concentrated on the remaining portion of their food.

Chapter 9

The Outside Perspective and the Future

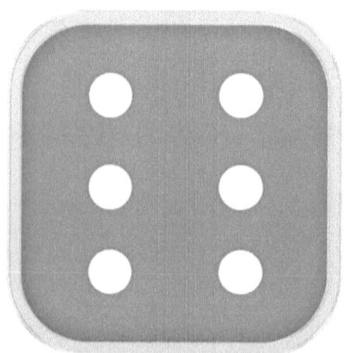

A braille sign

A group of disabled signs

Another braille sign

A challenged ear impaired sign

General Perspective Taken by the Normal Population

When members of the general public are asked about their knowledge of the CP, not much is learned from them. Usually the public see the challenged individuals around in the community, assisted by their family members or professional help. Ignorance about their behavior, which is sometimes perceived as aggressive, leads the general public to shy away from them or become anxious of their presence.

Again from the parents and guardian, for the most part, relate with empathy to their challenged children. They believe it is God's infinite design for them to have these challenged children, and like Texas mom, Krist Roberts, they will fight their utmost for the child to live a normal life.[42] Parents like Madam Quinn and Mrs. Williams believe the children are God's gift, so they naturally live their lives as they do with their other siblings. A few parents, particularly African parents, believe this is God's way of admonishing them for their sins. On the other hand, the African American parents of Zack are constantly fighting to ensure their son emerge a victor over his challenges.

Analyzing our communities, some members of the community have relatively more knowledge of the CP due to family ties, friends having a child with disabilities, or discussions with professionals in the field. This category has a better tolerance and can relate to the CP with empathy. Finally there is the small group that educates themselves about these challenged individuals through the literature that is now available from conventional means. Also, they obtain information from what presently exists in the electronic media and websites in general.

Only from my employment in this domain of the CP did I learn so much about them. By being very interested with this group, I continue to learn this much about them. My gratitude goes to the entities as well as the individuals who have contributed significantly in positively projecting the great work done in this field.

Most agencies have very informative websites, newsletters, journals, and publications centered on the challenged individuals. Networks of advocacy organizations relentlessly work to ensure the rights of the CP, which include their right for self-determination is upheld. Also, there are individuals who have made very impactful publications from which brilliant achievement done in this field could be read.

As could be seen for every population, we have their various segments, that is, from the least to the most endowed with special gifts.

---

[42] www.foxnews.com/us/2012/03/24/texsas/mom-plans-to-sue-school-district.

Paradoxically with the CP, I will simply say, among these segments is the celebrity group in the field that have been discovered and made popular by the media. In that respect, I will mention a few who will be interesting cases for reflection. This list could be interchangeable with the previous list in chapter five, depicting challenged individuals who contributed significantly to human endeavor. Here the focus is on their absolute resoluteness in overcoming their challenges.

In presenting an overview, I realize how this CP has been very inclusive and characterizes its spectrum with much diverse entities. The list includes members from our presidential families, politicians in general, intellectuals, the haves and have-nots, the youths and aged, ordinary folks, and individuals from all fields of human endeavors.

- Australian Nick Vujicic was born with no hand and legs. Despite these daunting challenges, he relentlessly battled to live his life to the fullest. It was quite amazing to see him walk up to the stage when he was called. An everyday task done by the average person was that spectacular when carried out by Nick, having such challenges.[43]
- Zach Anner has cerebral palsy. Known for his kind heart and humor, he submitted a video to the *Oprah Winfrey Show*, which eventually got him his own show.[44]
- Jes Sachse, a Canadian college student with a rare genetic condition known as Freeman-Sheldon syndrome, became a model for this population.[45]
- Stephen Hawking, the very popular professor, is famous for his black hole theories, and his only mobility comes from his head. He has become a blessing to our generation. With his endless reservoir of resilience, this physicist was able to leave a befitting legacy to this generation and many to come. His scientific work in the field qualifies him to be a true blessing to mankind.

---

[43] www.oprah.com/oprahs-lifeclass/How-Nick-Vujicic-Triumphed-Against-All-Odds.

[44] www.oprah.com/own-your-own-show/And-The-Winner-Of-your-Own-Show-Is.

[45] www.hollynorris.ca/americanable#h39067524.

Among other recognitions, he has been given twelve awards and honored as the greatest living scientist.[46]

- Richie Parker of Beaufort, South Carolina, is physically challenged, as he was born in May 1983 without arms. He extremely and graciously overcame his challenge to function efficiently in the society. He presently works for Hendricks Automobile Company as an automobile engineering technician, a subsidiary of NASCAR Motors. Interestingly he works and performs all his routine activities without any prosthetics, just simple innovative jigs and his formidable feet.[47]

- Helen Adams Keller was an American author, political activist, and lecturer. She was the first deaf and blind person to earn a bachelor of arts degree. The story of how Keller's teacher, Annie Sullivan, broke through the isolation imposed by a near complete lack of language, allowing the girl to blossom as she learned to communicate, has become known worldwide through the dramatic depictions of the play and film *The Miracle Worker*.[48]

- Jean-Do was a well-known French journalist, author, and editor of the French fashion magazine *Elle*. In 1995 he suffered a massive heart attack, causing him to go into a coma for twenty days. After coming out of the coma, he found himself with a very rare neurological disorder called locked-in syndrome, in which the mental state is perfectly normal and stable but the body is paralyzed from head to toe.[49] The left eyelid was the only moveable part of his body. With an extraordinary display of resoluteness, he wrote a book, *The Diving Bell and the Butterfly*. (Page 77/76 Yes the website www.studentpulse.com will also reference it. The source is Kar Yee Katherine Law3 (2011) Jean Dominique Bauby (Jean Do) wrote the Diving bell and the Butterfly. He was a victim of locked in Syndrome. Also Books June 15 1997)

---

[46] www.hawking.org.uk/the-computer.html; www.biography.com/people/stephen-hawking-933170.

[47] www.autoblog.com/2013/08/22richie-parker-nascar-no-arm-video.

[48] www.biography.com/people/hellen-keller-9361967.

[49] Kar Yee Katherine Law, 3 (2011)(03):1–2.

Two individuals worth mentioning at this point belong to the general populace who suddenly became disabled by sheer accident. A drunk driver hit the first; the second is a war veteran hurt in the line of duty. Both displayed their unbroken will to continue living their lives to the fullest. Again this confirms our vulnerability of being part of the CP.

- Kari Miller lost part of both legs unfortunately from a drunken driver. She lived to become a collegiate athlete and two-time Paralympics medalist. In 2008 she and her team won a silver medal in Beijing.[50]
- Steve Martin, an Afghanistan war veteran who was injured as a result of an improvised explosive device (IED), finally had his legs amputated after undergoing fourteen surgeries. Presently he is one of four double amputee police officers in the United States. His participation in several half marathons has contributed to other participants having more resoluteness in completing this endurable sport.[51]

The last Olympics showed how athletics with prosthetics challenged world records in track and field events. Oscar Pistorius of South Africa is an example of someone who amazingly competed with the best of this generation's athletes. In 2007 he was awarded the Helen Rollason BBC Sports Personality of the Year award, a special recognition for outstanding achievement in the face of adversity, an award that was received by both Sir Frank Williams of Formula One in 2010 and Martine Wright in 2012. Despite losing both legs in the 2005 London bombing, Ms. Wright was part of the Great Britain volleyball team at the London 2012 Paralympics.[52]

Similarly a disabled writer's club compiled literature for the late Elizabeth Boggs on her hundredth-year anniversary. All the poems and articles written there are so unique, touching, and full of wisdom. Reading this literature will truly resonate with our humanity.

---

[50] www.teamusa.org.

[51] www.disabledsportsusa.org/about-us/testimonials/athlete-profile-steve-martin.

[52] www.bbc.com/sport/0/sports-personality/30408734.

We learn about defiance from a mother of the disabled. Texas mom Krist Roberts refused to accept the decision made by the authorities of Kings Manor School of Kingwood, Texas, mandating that her child with cerebral palsy discontinue using her walker. She refused this judgment and eventually succeeded in proving them wrong. Stories of this nature are not uncommon in this population.[53]

At a recent DSP week in September 2014, I heard two touching stories:

- A consumer wanted to connect to his brother whom he had been estranged from for more than forty years. Fortunately a newly hired DSP working with him went to work with the little information given. With Facebook and other innovative means, he was able to find this long-lost brother, and in five minutes the two brothers were on the phone talking. Later a physical meeting was arranged in which they had dinner at the brother's place. A few months later, the long-lost brother called to say that he had been diagnosed with cancer a few weeks before they met. He passed away shortly after. But this timely intervention by the DSP brought the brothers together. The individual at the group home was left with memories, photos, and contacts to his other family members.

- Another consumer desired to meet the current pope. Again the DSP took up the challenge and started making an effort to achieve this goal, far-fetched as it might seem for some. The DSP worked with the individual for eight months toward that goal, and eventually he obtained pertinent information and resources, which got them to the Vatican in Rome. There, wishes of such nature, that is, to see the pope, was usually done by a lottery, considering the magnitude of request and practical availability of the pope. As providence would have it, the consumer did meet the pope, and he came to his group home. The consumer has a big picture of the pope and himself hanging in his room.[54]

---

[53] http://www.foxnews.com/us/2012/03/24/texas-mom-plans-to-sue-school-district-after-say.

[54] Mr. Momanyi, "Peter" to his agency workmates, shared both stories.

"Our challenged individuals celebrating life"

These inspiring stories do speak volumes, demonstrating what could be achieved when DSPs and all supporting members work diligently to improve the lives of our CP. Hence these efforts also help the inclusion that is required of them in our society. The list of celebrities in this field is long, simply because, as we look into their lives, we cannot help but realize the magnitude of their everyday challenges and how they fight to overcome them.

Albert J. Dunlap, a corporate executive, revolutionized Scott Paper. He increased the company's assets by millions of dollars. With this in mind, I believe readers will now, if not before, start realizing how the inclusion of the CP to the normal community should be a must.

Again we see how other celebrities like Celine Dion have touchingly embraced the CP as their ardent fans during their most acclaimed musical concert shows. In this spirit it is very refreshing to reference the Disability Pride Parade of Chicago. They see disability as a natural part of human diversity. As truly expressed by the parade, they are not asking for anything, and they are not complaining. They are showing their pride in being people, particularly individuals with disabilities.

Whatever can be done to bring that inclusion should be actively pursued. With a more holistic or rather universal understanding of this CP, individuals and entities have the opportunity to lend their support in the best way they can. The government arm has indeed given the needed support, but as always, the responsibility to steer the ship to a brighter shore rests on them.

Greater latitude of awareness should be a never-ending effort given to this population; therefore, television channels should help with more educational and entertaining materials of the CP. Indeed TV channel like 4HD have occasionally aired programs of the disabled, as they did cover Matheny prom activities.[55]

Other sources of media and publicity coverage have been of great help; however with additional audiovisual coverage, particularly from the TV networks, the impact will be felt. Also, state, county, and townships should have a percentage of CP programs through their network channels to make this outreach readily available to the general public.

I hope this traverse of the CP has been quite worthwhile for the readership, which I do sincerely appreciate. Information here should bring out more divergence in supporting the CP. This will eventually bring out the convergence in understanding our individually challenged. Whatever area or specialty the reader believes he or she can participate in will definitely help this population. This assistance will enable them to make choices, as we do on an everyday basis.

The journey has been to shed light on the CP and continue justifying their inclusion into the society at large. Again the readership will agree that the spectrum of the challenged people, when placed in perspective to the CP, becomes clearer with examples given.

In this spectrum of the challenged people, we see the deaf and dumb, the geriatric patients, patients incapacitated by accidents, our disabled veterans, the mentally challenged, and the complete group of our intellectually and physically challenged population. This humbly reminds us that we are all challenged in one way or the other; thus we will continue to be grateful for all God Almighty has done for us.

Lists for the Challenged Population
- List of medical stores selling adaptive equipments, wheelchairs, and prosthetics
- List of some individuals with disabilities that have distinguished themselves

---

[55] For more information, visit www.matheny.org; nevertheless more coverage should be done.

- List of supporting entities, for example, Elizabeth Boggs Center, Matheny Center, advocate groups, and so forth
- Glossary of words used by the CP
- List of some provider agencies in New Jersey and those out of state listed with DHS
- Government agencies and entities directly related to the CP
- References and further CP reading materials

List of Some Medical Stores Selling Adaptive Equipment and Wheelchairs in New Jersey and the United States

- Medical store in Sayreville, New Jersey, selling adaptive devices and other products used by the CP
- Freedomliftsystem.com 888 331 5621
- Burno stairlifts 888-545-4846 www.livingfreehome.com/bruno-stairlifts
- DynaVox support.na@tobiidynavox.com
- Sports shops
- Union Avenue Pharmacy, 433 West Union Avenue, Bound Brook, NJ 08805, (732) 893-7955, unionave@yahoo.com, www.unionavepharmacyclickforward.com
- AME Adaptive Medical Equipment, 8701 Broadway Street, Suite 101, Pearland, TX 77584, (866) 485-8881, info@adaptivemedical equipment.com, www.adaptivemedicalequipment.com
- North Coast-Medical & Rehabilitation Product, HQ-North Coast Medical, Inc., 8100 Camino Arroyo, Gilroy, CA 95020, www.ncmedical.com
- Acorn Stair lifts, Inc., 7335 Lake Ellenor Drive, Orlando, FL 32809, (866) 207-7554, www.acornstairlifts.com
- Invacare: phone 1.800.333.6900 Also local contacts: APRIA head THCARE group, 262 old New Brunswick road, Piscataway, NJ 08854
- Invacare Corporation: Worldwide Headquarters 1 Invacare Way, Elyria. OH 44035-4190 Phone:(800) 333-6900, Fax:(877) 619-7996

List of Some Individuals with disabilities who have distinguished themselves in human endeavors

- Adam Young, multi-instrumentalist, producer, and founder of the electronic project Owl City
- Adrian Lamo, American computer hacker
- Carl Soderholm, speaker in neuropsychiatric disorders
- Clay Marzo, American professional surfer
- Craig Nicholls, front man of the Vines, an Australian garage rock band
- Dan Aykroyd, comedian and actor[56]
- Heather Kuzmich, fashion model and reality show contestant on *America's Next Top Model*
- James Durbin, finalist on the tenth season of *American Idol*
- Jerry Newport, American author, mathematical savant, and basis of the film *Mozart and the Whale*
- John Elder Robison, author of *Look Me in the Eye*
- Michael Burry, American investment fund manager
- Tim Page, Pulitzer Prize–winning critic and author
- Travis Meeks, lead singer, guitarist, and songwriter for Days of the New, an acoustic rock band
- Vernon L. Smith, Nobel laureate in economics[57]
- Albert Einstein (1879–1955), German American theoretical physicist
- Alexander Graham Bell (1847–1922), American inventor of the telephone
- Emily Dickinson (1830–86), American poet
- Marilyn Monroe (1926–62), American actress
- H. P. Lovecraft (1890–1937), American writer
- Henry Ford (1863–1947), American industrialist
- Henry David Thoreau (1817–62), American writer
- Nikola Tesla (1856–1943), Serbian American scientist, engineer, and inventor of electric motors
- Robin Williams (1951–2014), American actor

---

[56] Aykroyd stated he has Asperger's, but some feel he was joking.
[57] He is speculated to have Asperger's syndrome.

Contemporary People

- Al Gore (1948–present), former American vice president and presidential candidate
- Bill Gates (1955–present), entrepreneur, philanthropist, and key player in the personal computer revolution
- Bob Dylan (1941–present), American singer/songwriter
- Charles Dickinson (1951–present), American writer
- Crispin Glover (1964–present), American actor
- James Taylor (1948–present), American singer/songwriter
- Oliver Sacks (1933–present), British American neurologist and author of *The Man Who Mistook His Wife for a Hat*

List of some Politicians and relatives with disabilities

- Father of United States of America 44th first lady, Michelle Obama, Fraser C Robinson 111, lived with multiple sclerosis, maintained a relationship and worked while raising a family. As narrated by his daughter, he developed multiple sclerosis as a young man. Born August 1 1935 in Chicago Illinois, married Marianne Shields also from Chicago, two children Craig and Michelle.

   He worked in the Chicago Water company and hardly missed a day even if he went to work using two canes. He died March 1991. **New York Times 11.08 2008**

- President Franklin Delano Roosevelt,(FDR) was the only President to enter office with a Physical disability in 1920.He was diagnosed with infantile paralysis, better known as polio in 1921 at the age of 39.He may also have been paralyzed by Guillain –Barre syndrome, GBS. www.fdrlibrary.marist.edu

- Rosemary Kennedy

   She was born 16 months after her brother John Fitzgerald Kennedy (JFK) was born with intellectual disabilities. Senior daughter of Joseph P Kennedy was born 1918 died January 7 2005.

   This urged Eunice Kennedy Shriver sister of JFK to make him contribute very much to developments towards the intellectual disabilities. In the twenty years that followed the Kennedy administration, congress passed 116 acts or amendments providing support for people with intellectual disabilities and their families.

- Established in 1966 by President Johnson the President's committee for people with disabilities (formally called the Presidential committee on mental retardation), was formed to provide advice to the President and the secretary of health and human services.
- Eunice Shriver continued to be dynamic and in 1968 founded the Special Olympics, an organization dedicated to celebrating and accepting people with disabilities as athletes. **(www. jfklibrary.org)**
- George Washington (1732–99), American politician
- Abraham Lincoln (1809–65), American politician
- Benjamin Franklin (1706–90), American politician/writer

Glossary of Words Usually Used by the Challenged Population

- **Advocacy:** the act or process of supporting a cause or proposal
- **Amyotrophic lateral sclerosis (ALS):** also known as Lou Gehrig's disease
- **Aneurysm:** an excessive, localized enlargement of artery caused by weakening of the artery wall
- **Angleman syndrome-** is a neuro-genetic disorder characterized by severe intellectual and developmental disability, sleep disturbance, seizures, jerky movements (especially hand-flapping), frequent laughter or smiling, and usually a happy demeanor
- **Aphasia:** the loss of ability to understand or express speech as a result of brain damage
- **Anoxia-** lack of oxygen supply, usually to the developing brain
- **Aneurysm-** an abnormal bulge or ballooning of blood vessel due to weakness of the wall or a damage to it
- **Apraxia:** the inability to perform particular purposeful actions as a result of brain damage
- **Autism:** a group of complex disorders of brain development characterized in varying degrees by difficulties in the social interaction, verbal and nonverbal communication, and repetitive behavior
- **Autism spectrum disorder:** a single disorder that includes disorders that were previously considered separate like autism,

Asperger's syndrome, and childhood disintegrative disorder, as now defined by the American Psychiatric Association Diagnosis (APAD) and Statistical Manual of Mental Disorder(DSM-5)

- **Bipolar** – a psychiatric disorder that causes extreme mood swings that include emotional highs (mania or hypomania) and lows (depression).
- **Asperger's syndrome:** a misunderstood and/or misdiagnosed disorder often characterized as having deficits in social skills, a reluctance to listen, a difficulty in understanding social give-and-take, and other core characteristics[58]
- **Bipolar II disorder:** a bipolar spectrum disorder that is characterized by at least one hypo manic episode and at least one major depressive episode and believed to be under diagnosed because hypomanic behavior often presents as high-functioning
- **Behavior issues-** Behavioral issues in children can lead to stress and frustration for the entire family. In young children, these issues may not yet be categorized as a specific diagnosis, but a child with significant behavioral issues may exhibit signs of anxiety, have frequent and severe tantrums, be manipulative, and/or be repetitively defiant towards those in authority
- **Brain injury-** damage to the brain from different cause
- **Fetal alcohol syndrome:** a disorder that is 100 percent preventable and could be reduced by 50 percent by using folic acid and vitamin B taken before and during the first two months of pregnancy[59]
- **Borderline personality disorder (BPD):** a personality disorder primarily characterized by emotional deregulations, extreme black-and-white thinking or splitting, and chaotic relationships, along with a pervasive instability in mood, interpersonal relationships, self-image, identity, and behavior
- **Cerebral palsy:** a disorder of movement, muscle tone, or posture that is caused by an injury to the immature developing brain most often before birth[60]

---

[58] www.autismspeaks.org.
[59] www.theracofsomerst.org/about/resources.
[60] www.mayoclinic.org.

- **Cognitive disabilities:** A variety of medical conditions affecting cognitive ability that leads to various intellectual or cognitive deficits.
- **Contract work:** This is work given to intellectually and developmentally challenge individuals, in their employment centers, for which they are paid for by their agencies.
- **Cornelia De Lange syndrome**- a syndrome of multiple congenital anomalies with distinctive facial appearance, prenatal and postnatal growth deficiency, feeding difficulties, psychomotor delay, behavioral problems, and associated malformations that mainly involve the upper extremities
- **Cortical visual impairment**- is a form of visual impairment that is caused by a brain problem rather than an eye problem
- **Down syndrome**- Genetic disability due to extra copy of chromosome 21, also called Trisomy 21
- **DSP:** Direct Support Professional
- **Dyslexia:** a reading disorder
- **Dysgraphia:** a disorder characterized by distorted and incorrect handwriting that it is often related to fine motor skills
- **Dyscalculia:** a disorder characterized by a problem with learning fundamentals that include one or more basic numerical skills
- **Dyspraxia (apraxia):**a condition characterized by a significant difficulty in carrying out routine tasks involving fine motor control and kinesthetic coordination (clumsy and uncoordinated movements)
- **EAP:** Employee Assistance program. A service provided by Health institutions and service providers in educating care givers about managing family challenges and other related isssues.
- **Encephalitis**- is inflammation of the brain
- **4qDeletion Syndrome**- Chromosome 4q Deletion Syndrome is a rare chromosomal disorder in which there is deletion of a portion of the 4th chromosome. Deletions may be in the middle of the chromosome arm ("interstitial") or at the end "terminal") and have varying effects.

- **Fibromyalgia:** a disorder characterized by widespread musculoskeletal pain accompanied by fatigue, sleep memory, and mood issues[61]
- **Fragile X syndrome-** Fragile X syndrome is a genetic condition that causes a range of developmental problems including learning disabilities and cognitive impairment. Usually, males are more severely affected by this disorder than females
- **Guillian Barre Syndrome, GBS:** A rapid onset muscle weakness as a result of damage to the peripheral nervous system.
- **Hypoxia-** is a condition in which the body or a region of the body is deprived of adequate oxygen supply.
- **Legally blind-** Legal blindness occurs when a person has central visual acuity (vision that allows a person to see straight ahead of them) of 20/200 or less in his or her better eye with correction. With 20/200 visual acuity, a person can see at 20 feet, what a person with 20/20 vision sees at 200 feet.
- **Lesch-Nyhamsyndrome-** is a condition that occurs almost exclusively in males. It is characterized by neurological and behavioral abnormalities and the overproduction of uric acid. Uric acid is a waste product of normal chemical processes and is found in blood and urine.
- **Lyn syndrome (spinal muscular atrophy)** - degeneration of motor neurons, the nerve cells in an area of the spinal cord known as the anterior horn
- **Mild mental retardation-** intellectual disability that exists in children whose brains do not develop properly or function within the normal range. There are four levels of retardation: mild, moderate, severe, and profound.
- **Multiple sclerosis-** Multiple sclerosis (MS) is a nervous system disease that affects your brain and spinal cord. It damages the myelin sheath, the material that surrounds and protects your nerve cells. This damage slows down or blocks messages between your brain and your body, leading to the symptoms of MS
- **ADHD:** attention deficiency hyperactivity disorder
- **ASL:** America Sign Language www.lifeprint.com/

---

[61] www.mayoclinic.org.

- **IHP:** Individual Habitation plan. A Comprehensive yearly pan of the consumer developed and reviewed by a support team. This includes but not limited to the Employment/Residential Manager, Case Manager, Family Member/guardian and the Consumer. Other support specialist e.g. the Resident Nurse and behavioral specialist could be included as deem fit.
- **ITD:** Inter Disciplinary Team. This team constitute of the Manager, Case manager, Family member and the consumers; other support specialist may join as deem fit.
- **Parkinson's disease-** Parkinson's disease is a progressive disorder of the nervous system that affects movement.
- **Rett syndrome-** is a neurodevelopmental disorder that affects girls almost exclusively. It is characterized by normal early growth and development followed by a slowing of development, loss of purposeful use of the hands, distinctive hand movements, slowed brain and head growth
- **RC:** Residential Counselor
- **Savant syndrome:** a condition in which a person with a mental disability, such as an autism spectrum disorder, demonstrates profound and prodigious capacities or abilities far in excess of what would be considered normal. A person affected with a mental disability (as autism or mental retardation) who exhibits exceptional skill or brilliance in some limited field (as mathematics or music) is also called "*savant.*"
- **Spina bifida-** is a birth defect where there is incomplete closing of the backbone and membranes around the spinal cord
- **Support system:** These are systems that complement the main system in caring out its objectives.
- **Tourette syndrome (Tourette's syndrome, Tourette's disorder, Gilles de la Tourette syndrome, GTS or, more commonly, simply Tourette's or TS):** an inherited neurological disorder with onset in childhood that is depicted by the presence of multiple physical (motor) tics and at least one vocal (phonic) tic that characteristically wax and wane. The exact cause is unknown, but it is well established that both genetic and environmental factors are involved.

- **Trinomy 13-** Trisomy 13, also called Patau syndrome, is a chromosomal condition associated with severe intellectual disability and physical abnormalities in many parts of the body
- **Traumatic brain injury**
- **Presidential Committee for People with Intellectual Disabilities (PCPID):** a group comprised of thirty-four members, including nineteen citizen members and thirteen ex officio (federal government) members. A maximum of twenty-one citizen members is allowed. The president appoints citizen members, and they serve for a maximum of two years. A variety of individuals are appointed as citizen members, including parents of individuals with intellectual disabilities, scientists, and professionals employed in the field of intellectual disabilities, community and business representatives, and systems advocates. The thirteen ex–officio members include the secretaries of Health and Human Services, Education, Labor, Housing and Urban Development, Commerce, Transportation, Interior, and Homeland Security; the U.S. Attorney General; the president and CEO of the Corporation for National and Community Service; the chair of the Equal Employment Opportunity Commission; the chair of the National Council on Disability; and the commissioner of the Social Security Administration. A team of federal employees support the committee.[62]

Some Provider Agencies in New Jersey and Outside the State

The Association of Retarded Citizens (ARC) has a rich history spanning sixty-plus years with great accomplishments. Started in 1950 by a small group of parents and concerned individuals, they decided to give these challenged individuals more than what the institutions offered. Like every parent, they wanted their children to live a fulfilled existence in the community, hence giving birth to the establishment of ARC.[63]

---

[62] U.S. Department of Health and Human Resources, www.acl.gov.
[63] www.thearc.org/ who-we-are/history.

- ARC Bergen-Passaic, (201) 343-0322, www.arcbp.com, Arc@ arcbp.com[64]ARC of Camden, 215 West White Horse Pike, Berlin, NJ 0809, (856) 767-3630, www.arccamdem.orgARC WAY Programs, www.arcwaysprograms.org
- Atlantic ARC, 6550 Delilah Road, Suite 101, Egg Harbor Township, NJ 08234, (609) 485-0800, http://arcatlantic.org
- Burlington ARC, 115 East Broad Street, Burlington NJ 08016, (856) 764-9494, www.arcofburlington.org[65]
- Cape May ARC, 822 Route 47, PO Box 225, South Dennis, NJ 08245, (609) 861-7100, http://arcofcapemay.org
- Cumberland ARC, 1680 West Sherman Avenue, Vineland, NJ 08360, (856) 691-9138, www.arccumberland.org[66]
- Essex ARC, 123 Nayon Avenue, Livingston, NJ 07039, (973) 535-1181, http://arcessex.org
- Gloucester ARC, 15555 Gateway Boulevard, West Deptford, NJ 08096, (856) 848-8648, info@thearcgloucester.orgThe ARC of Hunterdon County, www.archunterdon.org[67] The ARC of Middlesex, 219 Black Horse Lane, North Brunswick, NJ 08902, (732) 821-1199, www.arc-mddlesex.org[68]ARC of Mercer County, 850 North Hermitage Road, Hermitage, PA 16148, (724) 981-2950, mcar@mercerarc.org, www.mercerarc.org
- Morris ARC, 1 Executive Drive, Morris Plains, NJ 07950-0123, (773) 326-9750, info@arcmorris.org, www.arcmorris.org Ocean ARC, 815 Cider Bridge Avenue, Lakewood, NJ 08701-4932, (732) 363-3335, Info@arcocean.org, www.arcocean.org
- Salem ARC, 150 Salem-Woodstown Road, PO Box 5, Salem, NJ 08079, (856) 935-3600, http://arcsalem.com SCARC, 11

---

[64] They are affiliated with ARC of New Jersey and the ARC of the United States.

[65] They are also affiliated with the ARC of New Jersey and the ARC of the United States.

[66] After the tragic death of Bill Evanoff came Lewis Demaro to continue the dream.

[67] They are affiliated with the ARC of New Jersey and the ARC of the United States.

[68] They are affiliated with the ARC of New Jersey and the ARC of the United States.

US Route 206, Suite 100, Augusta, NJ 07822, (973) 383-7442, www.scarc.org

- Somerset ARC, 141 South Main Street, Manville, NJ 08835-1802, (908) 725-8544, Lawraz@thearcofSomerset.org, www.thearcofsomerset.orgUnion ARC, 70 Diamond Road, Springfield, NJ 07081, (973) 315-0000, info@arcunion.org, www.arcunion.orgWarren ARC, 319 West Washington Avenue, PO Box 389, Washington, NJ 07882, info@arcwarren.org, www.arcwarren.orgThe ARC of New Jersey, 985 Livingston Avenue, North Brunswick, NJ 08902, www.arcnj.org
- The ARC of the United States, 1010 Wayne Avenue, Suite 650, Silver Spring, MD 20910, (301) 565-3842, www.thearc.org

Service Providers Operating Schools

- Allegro School and Programs, 125 Ridgedale Avenue, Cedar Knolls, NJ 07927, (973) 539-1115, allegro1@msn.com, www.allegroschool.org
- Durand Academy and Community Service Special Education School, 230 North Evergreen Avenue, Woodbury, NJ 08096, (856) 235-3540, www.durandac.org / 111 Gaither Drive, Suite 101, Mount Laurel, NJ 08054
- Elwyn NJ, Elwyn, PA 19063, (610) 891-2000, info@elwyn.orgMatheny School and Hospital, 65 Highland Avenue, PO Box 339, Pea Pack, NJ 07977, (908) 234-0011, www.matheney.orgMidland Adult Services, 94 Reading Ton Road, PO Box 5026, North Branch, NJ 08876, (908) 722-8222, info@midlandschool.org, www.midlandschool.org/midland-adult-service
- Princeton Child Development Institute (PCDI), 300 Cold Soil Road, Princeton, NJ 08540, info@pcdi.orgSkyland Center, 145 Carleton Road, Ringwood, NJ 0756, Skylandcenter.orgWilloglen Academy, 628 Terrill Road, Plainfield, NJ 07062, (908) 561-5731
- Bethesda Lutheran Homes, 220 Hamburg Turnpike, Pompton Lakes, NJ 07442, (973) 831-4088

- Cooperate Center, 600 Hoffmann Drive, Watertown, WI, 53094, (800) 369-4636, www.bethesdalutherancommunities.org
- Cerebral Palsy Association Middlesex, Roosevelt Park 10 Oak Drive, Edison, NJ 08837, (732) 549-6187, www.cparmc.org
- Community Options, 16 Faber Road, Princeton, NJ 08540, (609) 951-9112, www.communityoptionsonline.org/jerseymercer Devereux, (610) 542-3031, www.devereux.org
- Our House, 76 Floral Avenue, Murray Hill, NJ 07974, (908) 464-8008
- Res-Care NJ, 900 Commerce Parkway, Suite A, Mount Laurel, NJ 08054-2234, (856) 608-8761

General Listing of Service Providers Mainly in New Jersey

- 1st CP of New Jersey, 7 Sanford Avenue, Belleville, NJ 07109-0710, (973) 751-0200, www.cerebralpalsycenter.org
- ABC Group Home
- Adept Programs Inc. in Brown Mills, 2320 Wrangle Hill Road, Suite 300, Burlington, NJ 08015Advoserv NJ, 2520 Rangel Hill Road, Suite 200, Beas, DE 19701
- Alfa Development
- Allies Inc., 1262 White Horse-Hamilton Square Road, Building A, Suite 101, Hamilton, NJ 08690, (609) 689-0136, www.alliesnj.org
- Bancroft Inc., 1255 Cadwell Road, Cherry Hill, NJ 08034, (888) 774-5516, Lynn.tomaio@bancroft.org
- Caring Inc., 407 West Delilah Road, Pleasantville, NJ 08232, (609) 641-0674, info@Caringinc.org, www.Caringinc.org
- El Roi Inc.
- Ladacin Network Inc.
- Opportunity Knocks Inc., 12 Dey Street, Englishtown, NJ 07726, (732) 446-6129
- Pafacom Inc., 1301 West Forest Grove Road, Building 3c, Vineland, NJ 08360, www.pafacom.org
- Alternatives, 600 1st Avenue, Raritan, NJ 08869, (908) 685-1444, www.alternatives.org
- Association of the Multiple Impaired Blind, Inc. (AMIB), 35 Beaverson Boulevard, Brick, NJ 08723, (732) 262-0082, www.oceanresourcenet.org

- Bethel Ridge, 175 South Maple Avenue, Basking Ridge, NJ 07920, (908) 221-0852, www.bethelridgenj.org, www.somersetcountymca.org
- Capitol Care, 185 Route 183, Stanhope, NJ 07874, (973) 426-1440, info@capitol-care.org, www.capitol-care.orgCareer OPP. Dev, 185 Route 183, Stanhope, NJ 07874, (973) 426-1440, info@stanhopecapitol-care.org
- Center for Humanistic Change New Jersey (CHCNJ), 12 US Highway 206, Stanhope, NJ 07874, http://chcnj.org
- Cerebral Palsy of North Jersey, 220 South Orange Avenue, Suite 300, Livingston, NJ 07039, (973) 763-9900, ext. 1100, dbishop@nj.org, www.cpnj.org
- Clifton Adult Opportunity CTR, 900 Clifton Avenue, Clifton, NJ 07013, (973) 777-7114
- Community Access Unlimited, (908) 354-3040, info@caunj.org, www.caunj.org
- Community Access for Independent Living, www.caunj.org
- Community Quest Inc., 6814 Tilton Road, Egg Harbor Township, NJ 08234
- Delta Community Supports, 2210 Mt. Carmel Avenue, Glenside, PA 19038, (215) 887-6300, www.deltaweb.orgDepartment for Persons with Disabilities
- Developmentally Disabled Association of New Jersey (DDANJ)
- Easter Seals Soc NJ, www.easterseals.com/nj
- Easter Seals New Jersey, 25 Kennedy Boulevard, Suite 600, East Brunswick, NJ 08816, (732) 257-6662
- Eastern Christian Children Retreat (ECCR), 700 Mountain Avenue, Wyckoff, NJ 07481, (201) 848-8005, www.eccretreat.org / 277 North Haledon Avenue, North Haledon, NJ 07508, (973) 427-8522
- Eden Acres
- Enable, 13 Roszel Road, Suite B110, Princeton, NJ 08540, (609) 987-5003, info@enablenj.org, www.enable.nj.orgEqual Partners, 774 Eayrestown, Lumberton, NJ 08048-3100, (609) 784-8475
- Family SVCS Burlington
- Burlington United Methodist Family services BUMFS

- Federation for the Multicultural Programs, 2 Van Sinderen Avenue, 2nd floor, Brooklyn, NY 11207, (718) 345-9500, http://webmail.fmcpny.org
- Hudson Milestones, 366-381 Clendenny Avenue, Jersey City, NJ 0304, (201) 434-7783, hedson.milestones@hudsonmilestones. org, www.hudsonmilestones.org
- Jewish Association for Developmental Disabilities (JADD), 190 Moore Street, Suite 272, Hackensack, NJ 07601-7418, (201) 457-0058, info@j-ADD.org, www.j-add.org/ video clip
- Jawonio, 260 North Little Tor Road, New City, NY 10956, lindly@haynes@jawonio.org, www.jawonio.org
- Jewish Services for the Developmentally Disabled (JSDD), 270 Pleasant Valley Way, PO Box 339, Western Orange, NJ 0703, www.jsddmetrowest.orgKelsch Associates Inc., 368 Broadway, Westville, NJ 08093, (856) 456-2022, www. kelschassociatesnj.netKeystone Community Living, 154 Front Street, South Plainfield, NJ 07080, (908) 757-1080, mail@ Keystonecomliving.com
- Life Opportunity Unlimited, 75 North Maple Avenue, Ridge World, NJ 07451, (201) 684-1128
- Life Skills Resource Center, 334 Elizabeth Avenue, Somerset, NJ 08873, (732) 805-0343
- Living in Freedom
- Lutheran Soc SVC, 640 South Broad Street, PO Box 8068, Trenton, NJ 08611, Mercercounty.org, www.nj.gov/counties/ mercerMiller Group HM
- National Institute for People with Disabilities, NIP/NJ Central Office, YAI Network, 460 West 34th Street, New York, NY 10001-2382, (212) 273-6100, http://supportyai.org
- New Concepts for Living, 68a West Passaic Street, Rachelle Park, NJ 07662, (201) 843-3427, info@ncfl.net, www.ncfl. netNew Horizons, 906 Rent 33, East Freehold, NJ 07728, (732) 998-0850, www.ahautism.orgNew Jersey Association for Deaf/ Blind
- Personalized Independent Living Opportunities Training (PILOT) Services, 289 Jackson Road, Berlin, NJ 08009, (856) 809-0600, thepilotservices@comcast.net

- Partnership for People, 23 Viceland Road, Suite 120, Florham Park, NJ 07932-1510, (973) 467-1648, pfp@ partnershipsforpeople.org, www.partnershipforpeople.org
- Prince Assoc, 106 North Garden Boulevard, Edgewater Park, NJ 08010, (609) 877-6920
- Promoting Specialized Conc Health (PSCH-NJ), 142-02 20th Avenue, 3rd floor, Flushing, NJ 113451, (778) 778-558
- QMANJ, 700 Cinnaminson Avenue, Building B, Palmyra, NJ 08065-2500, (856) 735-1011
- RAPHA, 18 Robbins Street, Toms River, NJ 08754, (732) 573-0358, info@raphainc.com
- Rem-NJ, 80 Cottontail Lane, Suite 330, Somerset, NJ 08873, (732) 552-2390
- Rose House, PO Box 544, Cedar Knolis, NJ 07227, (973) 984-0002, www.rosehouse.org
- Search Day Program, 73 Wickapecko Drive, Ocean, NJ 07712, (732) 531-0454, info@searchdayprogram.com, www.searchdayprogram.comSocial Educational/Residential/ Vocational (SERV) Behavior Health System, Inc., 20 Scotch Road, Ewing, NJ 08628, (609) 406-0125, www.servbhs. incSpecial Care Comm. SVCS, 17 May Court, Piscataway, NJ 08854-2413, (732) 752-4366
- Special Children Center, 1400 Prospect Street, Lakewood, NJ 08701
- Special Homes, 92 Broadway, Denville, NJ 07834
- Spectrum for Living, 210 River Vale Road, Suite 3, River Vale, NJ 07675
- Spectrum for Living, 200 Spectrum Drive, Edison, NJ 08817, (732) 287-FAX
- Twenty-One Plus, Inc., 252 Washington Street, Toms River, NJ 08753
- United Cerebral Palsy Hudson County
- United Cerebral Palsy of Northern, Central, and Southern New Jersey, www.ucp.org
- Universal Institute
- Venice Avenue

- Volunteers of America, 1660 Duke Street, Alexandria, VA 22314, (703) 341-5000
- Zion Presbyterian Church

List of Government Departments and Entities Directly Related to the Challenged Population

- **DHS:** Department of Human Services
- **DDD:** Division of Developmental Disabilities
- **ABCD:** The Alliance for the Betterment of Citizens with Disabilities.
- **AAMR:** American Association of Mental Retardation
- **ADRC:** Aging and Disability Resources Connection
- **ASPEN:** Asperger's Syndrome Education Network
- **AAIDD:** American Association on Intellectual and Developmental Disabilities[69]
- **CARF:** Commission on Accreditation of Rehabilitation Facilities
- **NDEAM:** National Disability Employment Awareness Month[70]
- **NIDRR:** National Institution Disability and Rehabilitation Research
- **ODEP:** Office of Disability Employment Policy[71]
- **AIDD:** Administration on Intellectual and Developmental Disabilities
- **PCPID:** Presidential Committee for People with Intellectual Disabilities
- **UCEDDs:** University Center for Excellence in Developmental Disability Education, Research, and Services
- **TASH:** The Association for Person with Severe Handicaps

---

[69] www.aaiddjournals.org.

[70] In 1945, it started as a weeklong program, and Congress expanded it in 1988 for a month. October is now recognized as the month (www.theracofsomeret.org).

[71] PCPID is a sub-Cabinet level policy agency under the U.S. Department of Labor. This organization develops and influences policies and practices that increase the number and quantity of employment opportunities for people with disabilities (www.dol.gov/odep/about).

- **The Task Force:** Instituted by President Clinton in 1998 with a bipartisan front, this group was followed by the Office of Disability Employment Policy.
- **ODEP:** Office of Disability Employment Policy[72]
- **Families of Spinal Muscular Atrophy (FSMA)**
- **LRE** Least Restrictive Environment
- **U.S. Department of Housing and Urban Development (HUD):** The Fair Housing Act prohibits discrimination by direct providers of housing, such as landlords, real estate companies, and other entities, such as banks, municipalities, or other lending institutions.
- **DOL:** Department of Labor[73]
- **New Jersey Council on Developmental and Disabilities (NJ CDD):** They ensure people with disabilities and their families become empowered advocates and participate in the design of services and support. They are more concerned in integrating to the society.[74]
- **Statewide Parent Advocacy Network (SPAN):** They carry early intervention services and are based in the state of New Jersey.
- **The ARC of New Jersey, Criminal Justice Advocacy Program (CJAP):** They provide alternatives to incarceration on behalf of individuals with developmental disabilities who are defendants in the criminal justice system. It is the only program of its kind.
- **NJDCA:** New Jersey Department of Community Affairs
- **NJHMFA:** New Jersey Housing and Mortgage Finance Agency
- **DCA:** Department of Community Affairs
- **Special Needs Housing Partnership Loan Program (SNHPLP):** Funding for this program comes from two agencies, the New Jersey Housing and Mortgage Finance Agency and the Department of Community Affairs. Each municipality can contribute Affordable Housing Trust Fund (AHTF) dollars toward SNHPLP projects. The New Jersey Housing and Mortgage Finance Agency and the Department of Community

---

[72] www.dol.gov/dol/media/webcast//20111214-odep/index.htm.

[73] www.dol.gov/dol/dol/media//2011/2014-odep/index.htm.

[74] PO Box 700, Trenton, NJ 08625-0700, (609) 292-3745, njcdd@njcdd.org, www.njcdd.org.

Affairs will match AHTF contributions on a dollar-to-dollar basis up to a maximum of $250,000 per project. In 2011, as part of one-time contributions, the NJHMFA gave $13 million, and the Department of Community Affairs donated $9 million to this program.

- **National Low Income Housing Coalition (NLIHC):** This group is solely dedicated to achieving socially, just public policy that assures people with the lowest incomes in the United States have affordable and decent homes.
- **National Housing Trust Fund (NHTF):** This group was established as a provision of the Housing and Economic Recovery Act of 2008, which President George W. Bush signed into law. The passage of this legislation is a major victory for low-income housing advocates and the lowest-income people in our country with the most serious needs.[75]
- **New Jersey Community Housing Partnership Programs (NJCHPP)**
- **Action DD:** This is the only disabilities advocacy group licensed in the state of Washington that receives no government money. Therefore, they are free to represent the best interests of people with developmental disabilities. Action DD leaders and volunteers receive no compensation.
- **Cerebral palsy of NJ**
- **The Epilepsy Foundation**
- **Recent background of The Central Registry:** The present establishment of the central registry of offenders against individuals with developmental disabilities reaffirms this meaningful change. The registry received bipartisan legislative support, and Governor Chris Christie signed it into law on April 30, 2010. It became effective on October 27, 2010 and exclusively applies to DHS-funded, licensed, contracted, or regulated programs that provide services with developmental disabilities, along with an office on autism (August 2010). The office promotes, disseminates, and coordinates best practices in the training of staff and other support to people with autism spectrum disorder (ASD) as well as autism awareness training

---

[75] nlihc.org/issues/nhtf.

to community entities. Acts pass by state. A few other legislative acts are promulgated by New Jersey. Acting Governor Kim Guadagno signed the legislation. This act was on increasing transportation safety for individuals with disabilities.

- Source America National Office, 8401 Old Court House Road, Vienna, VA 22182, (571) 226-4660, customerservice@source. org, www.SourceAmerica.org
- Source America East Region, 8320 Old Court House Road, Vienna, VA 22182, (703) 584-3923, eservices@ sourceamerica.org

    Source America (formerly NISH), is a national nonprofit, the leading source of job opportunities for a dedicated and highly qualified workforce, specifically people of significant disability. They make the American dream more accessible to a segment of the population where 80 percent do not have jobs.[76]

The U.S. Department of Health and Human Services Coordinates with the following:

- U.S. Department of Housing and Urban Development (HUD)
- U.S. Department of Education (ED)
- U.S. Department of Health and Human Services (HHS)
- U.S. Department of Labor (DOL)
- U.S. Department of Transportation (DOT)
- U.S. Department of the Treasury
- U.S. Department of Justice
- American Association on Intellectual and Developmental Disabilities
- National Association of Councils on Developmental Disabilities (NACDD)

---

[76] www.sourceamerica.org/about-us.

References

I sincerely appreciate the following entities and individuals, whose work in this field has brought more depth and clarity in understanding the CP.

- Elizabeth Boggs Center, www.elzabethboggscenter.org
- Matheny Medical and Educational Center, www.matheny center.org
- University of Medical and Dentistry of New Jersey (UMDNJ)
- AMS Vans Inc., America's mobility superstore
- Medicaid Program
- Invacare, an American manufacturer and distributor of nonacute medical equipment, including wheelchairs, mobility scooters, walkers, pressure care and positioning, and respiratory products. Invacare distributes to more than eighty countries around the world. Its present worth is over $1.8 billion.
- America Association on Intellectual and Developmental Disabilities (AAIDD) (www.aaiddjournals.org) has similar goals with other entities mentioned previously. They enhance the capacity of professionals who work with individuals with intellectual and developmental disabilities (training). For CP awareness, they promote the development of a society that fully includes individuals with IIDD. They sustain an effective responsive, well-managed, and responsibly governed organization. Also, they collaborate and partner with entities fostering similar goals.
- "Financial Struggles in the CP." Kira ARC of North Carolina uploaded a video on Social Security on upworthy.com. Here, Kira tell how she depends on SSI as a financial lifeline to etch a living. Though solvent until 2037, these programs are quickly becoming vulnerable to fiscal cuts.
- Sunrise Medicals leads in the design, manufacturing, and marketing of innovative, high-quality mobility products.

Sunrise Medical LTD, Thons Rd Brierley Hill West Midlands, DY5 2LD, United Kingdom
- Hope Haven International, 1800 19 Street, Rock Valley, IA 51247
- Arcon Stair Lifts, Inc., 7335 Lake Ellenor Drive, Orlando, FL 32809, (866) 207-7554, www.acronstairlifts.com
- Spinlife, experts in motion from which lifts, vehicle lifts, beds, and parts are sold, carries all the top brands, including Invacare, Sunrise Medical, Quickie, Pride Mobility, Drive Medical, TILite, ROHO, Medline, and many more[77]
- Direct Relief
- Free Wheelchair Foundation
- Freedom Lift System, freedomliftsystem.com
- 4Q-Mobility Works, 4199 Kinross Lakes Parkway, Suite 300, Richfield, OH 44286 (877) 275-4907 or (234) 312-200, mobilityworks.com
- Medicare Program, (800) Medicare or (800) 633-4227, www.medicare.gov
- Center for Medicare and Medicaid Services, Baltimore, MD 21244-1850
- Department of Human Services, Division of Developmental Disabilities
- Network of advocacy websites
- American Disabled for Attendant Programs Today (ADAPT) was organized by the Atlantis Community. They primarily serve the physically disabled and focus on advocating for rights and services.
- American Association on Intellectual and Developmental Disabilities
- American Association of People with Disabilities is a cross-disability organization that focuses on advocacy and services.
- American Coalition of Citizens with Disabilities
- American Council of the Blind
- American Diabetes Association
- American Foundation for the Blind primarily serves the blind population and focuses on advocacy and services.

---

[77] www.spinlife.com/about/contact.cfm, (800) 850-0335.

- ARC Association for Real Change
- The ARC of the United States is a national organization that serves people with intellectual and developmental disabilities.
- Aspies for Freedom
- Association of Programs for Rural Independent Living
- Autism National Committee
- Autism Network International
- Autistic Self-Advocacy Network is an international organization that provides support, services, and public policy advocacy for those on the autism spectrum while working to improve the public perception of autism and related conditions. It is run by autistic people and was founded by autistic self-advocates, Ari Ne'eman and Scott Robertson.
- Burton Blatt Institute
- Canadian National Institute for the Blind
- Community Alliance for the Ethical Treatment of Youth
- Center for Independent Living is an American organization that primarily serves the physically disabled and focuses on advocacy and services.
- Council of Parent Attorneys and Advocates
- Disabled American Veterans
- Disabled Children's Computer Group
- Disabled in Action is an American organization that primarily serves the physically disabled and focuses on advocacy and services. The group concerns itself with lobbying for new legislation that would provide for and defend the civil rights of people with disabilities and enforce current legislation.
- Disabled Peoples' International
- Disabled Women's Network Canada
- Disability Rights Commission
- Disability Rights Education and Defense Fund (DREDF)
- Dreams for Kids
- Enabling Unit ensures affirmative action concerning persons with disabilities at University College of Medical Sciences, Delhi. It is the first such unit for students with disabilities in any medical institution in India.

- Easter Seals, an international organization, provides services, education, outreach, and advocacy so people living with autism and other disabilities can live, learn, work, and play in their communities.
- Endeavour
- Equal Employment Opportunity Commission
- Finnish Association on Intellectual and Developmental Disabilities (FAIDD)
- Galloway's Society for the Blind
- Handicap International
- IDIRIYA is a nonprofit Sri Lankan NGO promoting "accessibility at public buildings and facilities and focusing on "accessible tourism for all."
- Indian Institute of Cerebral Palsy Kolkata
- Infinite Ability is a special interest group within the Medical Humanities Group of University College of Medical Sciences, Delhi, India. The group uses medical humanitarian approaches focusing on four competency-based learning objectives of narrative medicine: graphic medicine, interpersonal and communication skills, patient care, and professionalism.
- International Disability and Development Consortium (IDDC)
- International Blind Sports Federation
- International Ventilator Users Network
- Justice for All
- Landmine Survivors Network
- Latvian Association for Support of Disabled People
- L'Arche
- Mencap
- Mental Disability Advocacy Center (MDAC)
- Mind (the National Association for Mental Health, United Kingdom)
- MindFreedom International, a nonprofit international organization, unites one hundred sponsor and affiliate grassroots groups with thousands of individual members to win human rights and alternatives for people labeled with psychiatric disabilities.

- Movement for the Intellectually Disabled of Singapore (MINDS)
- Muscular Dystrophy Association
- National Alliance on Mental Illness
- National Association of the Deaf, an American organization, primarily serves the deaf population and focuses on advocacy and services.
- National Autistic Society
- Division of Medical Assistance and Health Services
- University Health Plan (UHP) Inc., NJ Family Care, provides affordable health coverage and quality care.
- Horizon NJ Health, Horizon Blue Cross Blue Shield of New Jersey
- Princeton Health Care System Employee Assistance Program, Heron Town Road, Princeton, NJ 08540, (800) 527-0035, ext. 1000
- The Initiative for Women with Disabilities (IWD)
- Elly & Steve Hammerman, Health Wellness Center, 359 2nd Avenue, New York, NY 10010
- **On Advocacy**: "No federal agency should define 'choice' so narrowly and illegally as to disenfranchise the most vulnerable segment of our disabled population," writes VOR (**Voice of the retarded**),in a plea to Congress to prohibit the use of U.S. Department of Health and Human Services (HHS) appropriations in support of deinstitutionalization activities. **Replaced below**
- VOR (Voice of the Retarded) supports advocacy groups by stating, "No federal agency should define 'choice' so narrowly and illegally as to disenfranchise the most vulnerable segment of our disabled population". This they write in a plea to congress to prohibit the use of U.S. Department of Human Services (HHS) appropriations in support of deinstitutionalization activities.
- Olmstead Decision of 1999.The US Supreme Court said that a state may not force people with disabilities to live apart from everyone else in order to get the service they need.
- Convention on the Rights of Persons with Disabilities, CRPD bipartisan vote of twelve to six on July 22, 2014.

Presidential Proclamation— National Disability Employment Awareness Month, 2014

NATIONAL DISABILITY EMPLOYMENT
AWARENESS MONTH, 2014

BY THE PRESIDENT OF THE UNITED STATES OF AMERICA

A PROCLAMATION

Americans with disabilities lead thriving businesses, teach our children, and serve our Nation; they are innovators and pioneers of technology. In urban centers and rural communities, they carry forward our Nation's legacy of hard work, responsibility, and sacrifice, and their contributions strengthen our economy and remind us that all Americans deserve the opportunity to participate fully in society. During National Disability Employment Awareness Month, we celebrate the Americans living with disabilities, including significant disabilities, who enrich our country, and we reaffirm the simple truth that each of us has something to give to the American story.

This year's theme, "Expect. Employ. Empower." reminds us that every American has a right to dignity, respect, and a fair shot at success in the workplace. For too long, workers with disabilities were measured by what people thought they could not do, depriving our Nation and economy of the full talents and contributions of millions of Americans. Nearly 25 years ago, the Americans with Disabilities Act codified the promise of an equal opportunity for everyone who worked hard, and in the years since, Americans with disabilities have reached extraordinary heights. But when employees with disabilities are passed over in the workplace or denied fair accommodations, it limits their potential and threatens our democracy; when disproportionate numbers of Americans with disabilities remain unemployed, more work must be done to achieve the spirit of what is one of the most comprehensive civil rights bills in the history of our country.

My Administration remains committed to tearing down the barriers that prevent Americans with disabilities from living fully independent, integrated lives. We have supported programs that more effectively prepare workers, including those with disabilities, for high-growth, high-demand careers, and we have found new ways to encourage businesses to foster flexible workplaces that are open to diverse skills. We are also working to ensure those living with disabilities have access to the resources that support employment, including accessible housing, transportation, and technology.

Meaningful careers not only provide ladders of opportunity into the middle class, but they also give us a sense of purpose and self-worth. When Americans with disabilities live without the fear of discrimination, they are free to make of their lives what they will. This month, we renew our commitment to cultivate a more inclusive workforce, and we continue our efforts to build a society where everyone who works hard has a chance to get ahead.

NOW, THEREFORE, I, BARACK OBAMA, President of the United States of America, by virtue of the authority vested in me by the Constitution and the laws of the United States do hereby proclaim October 2014 as National Disability Employment Awareness Month. I urge all Americans to embrace the talents and skills that individuals with disabilities bring to our workplaces and communities and to promote the right to equal employment opportunity for all people.

IN WITNESS WHEREOF, I have hereunto set my hand this thirtieth day of September, in the year of our Lord two thousand fourteen, and of the Independence of the United States of America the two hundred and thirty-ninth.[78]

—Barack Obama

---

[78] www.whitehouse.gov/the-press-office/2014/09/30/presidential-national.

Presidential Proclamation -- National Disability Employment Awareness Month, 2015

NATIONAL DISABILITY EMPLOYMENT AWARENESS MONTH, 2015

- - - - - - -

BY THE PRESIDENT OF THE UNITED STATES OF AMERICA A PROCLAMATION

A quarter century ago, our country took a major step toward fulfilling the fundamental American promises of equal access, equal opportunity, and equal respect for all when the Americans with Disabilities Act (ADA) was made the law of the land. While we have continued to make advancements that help uphold this basic belief, we must address the injustices that remain. During National Disability Employment Awareness Month, we celebrate the ways individuals with disabilities strengthen our workforce, our communities, and our country, and we recommit to cultivating an America where all people are able to build vibrant futures for themselves and for their families.

Americans with disabilities make up almost one-fifth of our population, but are unemployed at a rate that is twice that of people without disabilities; and for women and minorities with disabilities, the rates are even higher. Despite all they contribute to our society, people with disabilities still face discrimination by employers, limited access to skills training, and, too often, unfairly low expectations. As a Nation, we must continue to promote inclusion in the workplace and to tear down the barriers that remain -- in hearts, in minds, and in policies -- to the security and prosperity that stable jobs provide and that all our people deserve. And we must actively foster a culture in which individuals are supported and accepted for who they are and in which it is okay to disclose one's disability without fear of discrimination.

My Administration is working to make sure our country does not let the incredible talents of Americans with disabilities go to waste.

We are working to strengthen protections against disability-based discrimination in the workplace and to expand employment possibilities for people with disabilities -- and the Federal Government is leading by example. I have taken action to require agencies and Federal contractors to hire more people with disabilities -- and thanks to these efforts, more Americans with disabilities are in Federal service than at any point in the last three decades.

I will continue fighting to widen pathways to opportunity for individuals with disabilities and supporting employers in their efforts to increase disability inclusion. The White House hosted a Summit on Disability and Employment earlier this year to provide businesses, philanthropies, and advocates with information on Federal resources for hiring disabled individuals. Last year, I was proud to sign the Workforce Innovation and Opportunity Act (WIOA), which encourages greater coordination across Federal, State, and local programs to expand access to high-quality workforce, education, and rehabilitation services. WIOA also helps youth with disabilities to receive extensive pre-employment transition services so they can find positions alongside people without disabilities and get paid above minimum wage. Additionally, last year I signed the Achieving a Better Life Experience (ABLE) Act, which allows eligible people with disabilities to establish tax-free savings accounts.

America is at its strongest when we harness the talents and celebrate the distinct gifts of all our people. This October, as we observe the 70th anniversary of National Disability Employment Awareness Month, let us pay tribute to all who fought for better laws, demanded better treatment, and overcame ignorance and indifference to make our Nation more perfect. In their honor, and for the betterment of generations of Americans to come, let us continue the work of removing obstacles to employment so every American has the chance to develop their skills and make their unique mark on the world we share.

NOW, THEREFORE, I, BARACK OBAMA, President of the United States of America, by virtue of the authority vested in me by the Constitution and the laws of the United States, do hereby proclaim October 2015 as National Disability Employment Awareness Month. I urge all Americans to embrace the talents and skills that individuals with disabilities bring to our workplaces and communities and to promote the right to equal employment opportunity for all people.

IN WITNESS WHEREOF, I have hereunto set my hand this thirtieth day of September, in the year of our Lord two thousand fifteen, and of the Independence of the United States of America the two hundred and fortieth.

BARACK OBAMA

Index

www.ingramcontent.com/pod-product-compliance
Lightning Source LLC
Chambersburg PA
CBHW020540290526
45786CB00002B/968